LONERGAN

OUTSTANDING CHRISTIAN THINKERS

Series Editor: Brian Davies OP

The series offers a range of authoritative studies on people who have made an outstanding contribution to Christian thought and understanding. The series will range across the full spectrum of Christian thought to include Catholic and Protestant thinkers, to cover East and West, historical and contemporary figures. By and large, each volume will focus on a single 'thinker', but occasionally the subject may be a movement or a school of thought.

Brian Davies OP, the Series Editor, is Regent of Studies at Blackfriars, Oxford, where he also teaches philosophy. He is a member of the Theology Faculty at the University of Oxford and tutor at St Benet's Hall, Oxford. He has lectured regularly at the University of Bristol, Fordham University, New York, and the Beda College, Rome. He is Reviews Editor of *New Blackfriars*. His previous publications include: *An Introduction to the Philosophy of Religion* (OUP, 1982); *Thinking about God* (Geoffrey Chapman, 1985); *The Thought of Thomas Aquinas* (OUP, 1992); and he was editor of *Language, Meaning and God* (Geoffrey Chapman, 1987).

Already published:

The Apostolic Fathers
Simon Tugwell OP

Denys the Areopagite
Andrew Louth

The Venerable Bede
Benedicta Ward SLG

Anselm
G. R. Evans

Teresa of Avila
Rowan Williams

Handel
Hamish Swanston

Bultmann
David Fergusson

Reinhold Niebuhr
Kenneth Durkin

Karl Rahner
William V. Dych SJ

Lonergan
Frederick E. Crowe SJ

Hans Urs von Balthasar
John O'Donnell SJ

Yves Congar
Aidan Nichols OP

Planned titles in the series include:

Jonathan Edwards
John E. Smith

LONERGAN

Frederick E. Crowe SJ

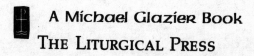
A Michael Glazier Book
THE LITURGICAL PRESS

A Michael Glazier Book
published by The Liturgical Press
St John's Abbey, Collegeville, MN 56321, USA

© Frederick E. Crowe SJ 1992

Published in Great Britain by Geoffrey Chapman, an imprint of
Cassell Publishers Limited
First published 1992

Library of Congress Cataloging-in-Publication Data
A catalog record for this book is available from the Library of Congress.

ISBN 0-8146-5052-X

Typeset by Colset Private Limited, Singapore
Printed and bound in Great Britain by
Biddles Ltd, Guildford and King's Lynn

Contents

Editorial foreword

St Anselm of Canterbury once described himself as someone with
faith seeking understanding. In words addressed to God he says 'I
long to understand in some degree thy truth, which my heart believes
and loves. For I do not seek to understand that I may believe, but I
believe in order to understand.'

And this is what Christians have always inevitably said, either
explicitly or implicitly. Christianity rests on faith, but it also has
content. It teaches and proclaims a distinctive and challenging view
of reality. It naturally encourages reflection. It is something to
think about; something about which one might even have second
thoughts.

But what have the greatest Christian thinkers said? And is it worth
saying? Does it engage with modern problems? Does it provide us
with a vision to live by? Does it make sense? Can it be preached? Is it
believable?

This series originates with questions like these in mind. Written by
experts, it aims to provide clear, authoritative and critical accounts
of outstanding Christian writers from New Testament times to the
present. It will range across the full spectrum of Christian thought to
include Catholic and Protestant thinkers, thinkers from East and
West, thinkers ancient, mediaeval and modern.

The series draws on the best scholarship currently available, so
it will interest all with a professional concern for the history of
Christian ideas. But contributors will also be writing for general
readers who have little or no previous knowledge of the subjects to
be dealt with. Volumes to appear should therefore prove helpful at a
popular as well as an academic level. For the most part they will be
devoted to a single thinker, but occasionally the subject will be a
movement or school of thought.

The subject of the present volume, though he has been described as a 'loner', is undoubtedly one of the most significant of twentieth-century Roman Catholic teachers and authors. Both traditional and modern, with concerns both theoretical and practical, he has been compared with Thomas Aquinas, on whom he commented and whose influence on him was considerable. Though verdicts on him vary, it is difficult to be justified in ignoring him, or in denying that he will be studied for a long time to come. The range of his interests and the sheer intellectual force of his literary output cannot but command respect and interest in serious-minded thinkers concerned, not only with theology and philosophy, in which Lonergan specialized, but also with the human sciences and with human studies in general.

Fr Frederick Crowe SJ is uniquely qualified to introduce readers to the work of Lonergan. A close friend of Lonergan, he has devoted more than 40 years of study to Lonergan's achievement. As befits his subject matter, and drawing on the vast amount of material available to him, Fr Crowe's approach is chronological and not simply thematic. Readers of his book will therefore find themselves learning about the development of an extraordinary mind from one of its leading exponents.

Brian Davies O P

Preface

A volume in an Outstanding Christian Thinkers series will naturally be concerned rather with the ideas of the thinker in question than with biography, and that is the case in this study of Bernard Lonergan. Still, in Newman's much-quoted phrase, to live is to change; if, then, thinkers keep on thinking, their ideas will keep on changing—genetically or dialectically, to use two of Lonergan's favourite terms—and so a choice has to be made between a systematic presentation of a final position and a chronological presentation of a developing mind.

I had no trouble setting the former aside. It does not correspond closely to Lonergan's way of thinking, which was more concerned with guiding future study and less with establishing systems in the present. Furthermore, while his students debate with one another the extent and significance of his development, my own view is that its magnitude still escapes us, and will escape us as long as we are in the stage, far from finished, of 'reaching up' to his mind. In any case my own study of Lonergan for several years has focused on his development, and so inevitably involves chronology.

There is a difficulty here in that we lack a biography of Lonergan. Excellent spadework is being done in preparation for a volume on his life, and I would have been happy to delay my own study till a biography was available. But on one side publishers have their schedule, and on the other I could not at my age plan for a volume five years from now. Already the normal difficulty of remembering in Chapter 6 what I wrote in Chapter 2 has increased immensely. So I have followed a chronological order, and indicated the transitional events, but only sketched the background that a biographer, we hope, will soon describe in detail.

A few aspects of my study may be mentioned, to keep readers

from expecting too much. It is rather personal at times—inevitable when my own career in theology has been interwoven with Lonergan's from the beginning. It no doubt betrays as well an advocacy of his ideas—inevitable again in one who finds it more profitable to learn from Lonergan than to search for blemishes in his work. It is more a monologue than a dialogue; I have seen most of the five thousand or more items of secondary literature collected in our Lonergan Research Institute, and may unconsciously have drawn on some of them (if so, my blanket acknowledgement and thanks to such sources), but limitations in both time and space prevented me from taking account of them. There is a parallel singleness of view and purpose in my neglect of Lonergan's relation to other thinkers; he was a loner, and must be studied in himself and for his own creative contribution; when that basis is laid, one could make interesting comparisons with other historical figures—but again it would take time and space, even supposing a familiarity that I do not possess with those figures.

So here is another book on Lonergan. I suppose no one who writes in this Outstanding Christian Thinkers series will pretend to be a substitute for those thinkers themselves. What we are attempting is to guide our readers into and through the works we present only in outline here. Once readers accept that guidance and achieve familiarity with the original thinkers themselves, they should find our presentations much less interesting. For that reason especially, I am grateful to Robert C. Croken and Gregory H. Carruthers, who undertook to check my work, at the expense of going over ground that is largely familiar to them.

March 1991

Bibliography

Bernard Lonergan's works: A selection

Collection, ed. F.E. Crowe and R.M. Doran (2nd edn; *Collected Works of Bernard Lonergan* 4; Toronto, 1988).

De Constitutione Christi Ontologica et Psychologica (Rome, 1956).

De Deo Trino, 2 vols (Rome, 1964) (vol. 1, 3rd edn; vol. 2, 2nd edn).

De Verbo Incarnato (3rd edn; Rome, 1964).

Grace and Freedom: Operative Grace in the Thought of St. Thomas Aquinas, ed. J.P. Burns (London/New York, 1971).

'The *Gratia Operans* dissertation: preface and introduction', *Method: Journal of Lonergan Studies* 3/2 (October 1985), pp. 9–46.

Insight: A Study of Human Understanding (2nd edn; London/New York, 1958).

Method in Theology (London/New York, 1972).

Philosophy of God, and Theology: The Relationship between Philosophy of God and the Functional Specialty, Systematics (St Michael's Lectures, Gonzaga University, Spokane, 1972; London/Philadelphia, 1973).

A Second Collection, ed. W. Ryan and B. Tyrrell (London/Philadelphia, 1974/1975).

A Third Collection, ed. F.E. Crowe (New York/London, 1985).

Three Lectures (Montreal, 1975).

Understanding and Being: The Halifax Lectures on Insight (2nd edn; *Collected Works of Bernard Lonergan* 5, ed. E. Morelli and M. Morelli, rev. and augmented by F.E. Crowe, with the collaboration of E. Morelli, M. Morelli, R. Doran and T. Daly; Toronto, 1990).

Verbum: Word and Idea in Aquinas, ed. D. Burrell (Notre Dame, IN/London, 1967/1968).

The Way to Nicea: The Dialectical Development of Trinitarian Theology (London/Philadelphia, 1976). Translation by C. O'Donovan of pp. 17–112, *Pars Dogmatica*, of *De Deo Trino* (Rome, 1964).

P. Lambert, C. Tansey and C. Going (eds), *Caring about Meaning: Patterns in the Life of Bernard Lonergan* (Montreal, 1982). (Transcribed from interviews: see below, p. 29, note 4.)

Selected Other Works

M. Beuchot, *Conocimiento, causalidad y metafísica* (Xalapa, Mexico, 1987).

F.P. Braio, *Lonergan's Retrieval of the Notion of Human Being: Clarifications of and Reflections on the Argument of Insight, Chapters I–XVIII* (Lanham, MD, 1988).

W.E. Conn, *Conscience: Development and Self-Transcendence* (Birmingham, AL, 1981).

P. Corcoran (ed.), *Looking at Lonergan's Method* (Dublin, 1975).

F.E. Crowe, *Appropriating the Lonergan Idea*, ed. Michael Vertin (Washington, DC, 1989).
The Lonergan Enterprise (Cambridge, MA, 1980).
(ed.), *Spirit as Inquiry: Studies in Honor of Bernard Lonergan* (Chicago, 1964).

W.J. Danaher, *Insight in Chemistry* (Lanham, MD, 1989).

R.M. Doran, *Psychic Conversion and Theological Foundations: Toward a Reorientation of the Human Sciences* (Chico, CA, 1981).
Theology and the Dialectics of History (Toronto, 1990).

T. Dunne, *Lonergan and Spirituality: Towards a Spiritual Integration* (Chicago, 1985).

W.R. Eidle, *The Self-Appropriation of Interiority: A Foundation for Psychology* (New York/Bern, 1990).

T.P. Fallon and P.B. Riley (eds), *Religion and Culture: Essays in Honor of Bernard Lonergan, S.J.* (Albany, NY, 1987).
(eds), *Religion in Context: Recent Studies in Lonergan* (Lanham, MD, 1988).

P. Fluri, *Einsicht in INSIGHT: Bernard J.F. Lonergans kritische-realistische Wissenschafts- und Erkenntnistheorie* (Frankfurt am Main, 1988).

D. Granfield, *The Inner Experience of Law: A Jurisprudence of Subjectivity* (Washington, DC, 1989).

V. Gregson, *Lonergan, Spirituality, and the Meeting of Religions* (Lanham, MD, 1985).

(ed.), *The Desires of the Human Heart: An Introduction to the Theology of Bernard Lonergan* (New York, 1988).

J. Heesh and N. Ormerod (eds), *Lonergan and You: An Australian Collaboration* (Riverview Reflections 1985; Sydney, 1987).

C. Hefling, *Why Doctrines?* (Cambridge, MA, 1984).

D. A. Helminiak, *The Same Jesus: A Contemporary Christology* (Chicago, 1986).

Spiritual Development: An Interdisciplinary Study (Chicago, 1987).

W. LaCentra, *The Authentic Self: Toward a Philosophy of Personality* (New York/Bern, 1987).

M. L. Lamb, *History, Method, and Theology: A Dialectical Comparison of Wilhelm Dilthey's Critique of Historical Reason and Bernard Lonergan's Meta-Methodology* (Missoula, MT, 1978).

Solidarity with Victims: Toward a Theology of Social Transformation (New York, 1982).

(ed.), *Creativity and Method: Essays in Honor of Bernard Lonergan, S. J.* (Milwaukee, 1981).

F. Lawrence (ed.), *Lonergan Workshop* (Atlanta, GA; 8 vols now in print, besides 3 supplementary vols).

D. Lenfers, *Search for Truth: A Student's Manual of Epistemology* (Adigrat, Ethiopia, 1982; distributed by White Fathers, Cologne, Germany).

Lonergan Research Institute, *Lonergan Studies Newsletter* (Toronto, 1980–   ).

B. Lovett, *Life Before Death: Inculturating Hope* (Quezon City, 1986).

On Earth as in Heaven: Corresponding to God in Philippine Context (Quezon City, 1988).

M. H. McCarthy, *The Crisis of Philosophy* (Albany, NY, 1989).

S. E. McEvenue and B. F. Meyer (eds), *Lonergan's Hermeneutics: Its Development and Application* (Washington, DC, 1989).

P. McShane, *Lonergan's Challenge to the University and the Economy* (Washington, DC, 1980).

Music That Is Soundless: An Introduction to God for the Graduate (2nd edn; Washington, DC, 1977).

Plants and Pianos: Two Essays in Advanced Methodology (Dublin, 1971).

Randomness, Statistics and Emergence (Dublin/London, 1970).

The Shaping of the Foundations: Being at Home in the Transcendental Method (Washington, DC, 1977).

Wealth of Self and Wealth of Nations: Self-Axis of the Great Ascent (Hicksville, NY, 1975).

(ed.), *Foundations of Theology: Papers from the International Lonergan Congress 1970* (Dublin/London/Notre Dame, 1971).

(ed.), *Language Truth and Meaning: Papers from the International Lonergan Congress 1970* (Dublin/London/Notre Dame, 1972).

(ed.), *Searching for Cultural Foundations* (Lanham, MD, 1984).

E. L. Mascall, *Nature and Supernature* (St Michael's Lectures, Gonzaga University, Spokane, 1973; London, 1976).

M. J. Matustik, *Mediation of Deconstruction: Bernard Lonergan's Method in Philosophy* (Lanham, MD, 1988).

K. F. Melchin, *History, Ethics, and Emergent Probability: Ethics, Society and History in the Work of Bernard Lonergan* (Lanham, MD, 1987).

B. F. Meyer, *Critical Realism and the New Testament* (Princeton Theological Monograph Series, Allison Park, PA, 1989).

H. A. Meynell, *An Introduction to the Philosophy of Bernard Lonergan* (London, 1976).

The Theology of Bernard Lonergan (Atlanta, GA, 1986).

E. A. Morelli, *Anxiety: A Study of the Affectivity of Moral Consciousness* (Lanham, MD, 1985).

M. D. Morelli, *Philosophy's Place in Culture: A Model* (Lanham, MD, 1984).

(ed.), *Method: Journal of Lonergan Studies* (Los Angeles, 1983–).

M. O'Callaghan, *Unity in Theology: Lonergan's Framework for Theology in Its New Context* (Washington, DC, 1980).

E. Pérez Valera, *El método cognoscitivo en Bernard Lonergan* (Mexico City, 1989).

V. Pérez Valera (ed.), *Humanidades Anuario* 10 (Mexico City, 1987)—issue devoted to studies of Lonergan.

M. Rende, *Lonergan on Conversion: Development of a Notion* (Lanham, MD, 1991).

G. B. Sala, *Das Apriori in der menschlichen Erkenntnis. Eine Studie über Kants Kritik der reinen Vernunft und Lonergans Insight* (Monographien zur philosophischen Forschung 97; Meisenheim am Glan, 1971).

'La métaphysique comme structure heuristique selon Bernard Lonergan', *Archives de Philosophie* 33 (1970), pp. 45–71; 35 (1972), pp. 443–67, 555–70; 36 (1973), pp. 43–68, 625–42.

T. Tekippe (ed.), *Papal Infallibility: An Application of Lonergan's Theological Method* (Washington, DC, 1983).

(ed.), *Primary Bibliography of Lonergan Sources* (3rd edn; New Orleans, 1988).

(ed.), *Secondary Bibliography of Lonergan Sources* (New Orleans, 1988).

D. Tracy, *The Achievement of Bernard Lonergan* (New York, 1970).

B. J. Tyrrell, *Bernard Lonergan's Philosophy of God* (Notre Dame, 1974).

E. Webb, *Philosophers of Consciousness: Polanyi, Lonergan, Voegelin, Ricoeur, Girard, Kierkegaard* (Seattle, 1988).

W. L. Ysaac (ed.), *The Third World and Bernard Lonergan: A Tribute to a Concerned Thinker* (Manila, 1986).

1

The remote context: home, studies, formation

Great and fundamental ideas are relevant everywhere, just as much to the work of those who conceived them as to that of others. If the ideas of Bernard Lonergan are of this depth and generality, one may use them in the study of his own life and thought. That is my justification for beginning this book with a brief account of his notion of context. I wish to examine the context which gives perspective to his work; to that end some idea of what context means should be helpful; and I find this in his own writings.

Context, he says, 'is a remainder-concept: it denotes the rest that is relevant to the interpretation of the text'. It may be a material context, 'the rest of the documents or monuments relevant to an interpretation'. But it may also be formal, and this has a hermeneutical aspect as well as a historical; the former is 'the dynamic mental and psychic background from which the author spoke or wrote . . . the set of habits of sensibility and skill, of intellect and will, that come to second act in the text'; the latter is 'the genetico-dialectical unity of a series of hermeneutic formal contexts'.[1]

On this view, it would be a mistake to start our exposition of Lonergan's thought where his academic career begins, with his doctoral dissertation of 1940 and the ideas he got from Thomas Aquinas. The works of Thomas and other authors would pertain to the material context, but the formal context is all the wealth of data and ideas, of judgements and values, of feelings and objectives, of language and memory—the whole store of experience in the widest

1

possible sense of that word, that constitutes 'the dynamic mental and psychic background from which' he wrote at any time. Further, as time passes the formal context changes, and so in his own life there is 'the genetico-dialectical unity of a series' of such formal contexts, not to mention the much longer series constituted by many lives and an age-old tradition.[2]

It follows that a significant part of Lonergan's context was constituted in the 34 years before he began his doctoral studies. The child is father to the man, and the youthful essayist to the mature lecturer. The ascetical training of Lonergan's youth, supporting him in the frustration of what his religious Order calls 'regency' years, sheds light on the self-transcendence that is intrinsic to his thinking on religion and theology. Again, the self-taught style of his formation is surely a factor in the individualist character of that later work. Yet again, his almost accidental introduction to the study of Thomas Aquinas has to be seen as a strange break between his bright dreams in the 1930s and the appearance of *Insight* in 1957. And it seems more than just a guess that the methods of prayer he learned from Ignatius Loyola contributed to an idea that dominated most of his life—the Ignatian vision of God operating always and everywhere and in all things—and gave him the serenity to do what needed doing and to be willing to wait for a later century to justify his strategy. From many viewpoints, then, it seems that a study of his work cannot dispense with the context of his youthful formation.

It happens also that this part of Lonergan's life was virtually unknown to the public during most of his career. Toward its close, however, interviewers were able to lift the veil a little, some of his own publications began to offer hints, and now some years after his death surviving letters and papers are available to give us information, glimpses only but very precious, of those early years. Relying on these sources and on personal memories, I will provide in this opening chapter, not the detail that a biographer would require, but at least a set of headings that will help to explain what would otherwise appear on the scene like Melchizedek, without known origin: the intrusion of piety, say, or character traits closely bound up with his later work, or strongly expressed feelings that all of a sudden appear in the text, or reflections that seem to come out of the blue, and so on.

THE LONERGAN FAMILY

The Lonergans were Irish immigrants to Canada in the early 1800s. Bernard's grandfather, Michael, lived with his wife Frances (Gorman, also of Irish extraction), first on a farm three miles upriver from Buckingham, Quebec, later in the town itself, where he ran a butcher's shop. Bernard's father, Gerald, went to university to study engineering, qualified as a surveyor, and spent his working life, except for the winters, mapping the western provinces of Canada. On the maternal side, Bernard was descended from English stock via United Empire Loyalists who came to Canada after the American revolution. It is interesting that on this side Bernard owed his existence to the size of nineteenth-century families, for his grandfather was the youngest of five children, his grandmother the twelfth of seventeen, and his mother the fifth of six. The grandparents were Hiram Wood and Jane Harrison, who lived first in Osnabruck township in eastern Ontario, then moved to Buckingham, where Hiram, a carpenter, practised the trade of millwright. It was here that Gerald Lonergan met their daughter Josephine Helen. They were married on 16 February 1904. Josephine went westward with her husband on his summer survey work, returned pregnant in the fall, to give birth to Bernard in her parents' home on 17 December of the same year. Bernard was followed in due course by his brothers Gregory and Mark—there were only the three children in the family.[3]

Canadian inland settlement was determined by the rivers of the country and their waterfalls. Buckingham was a milltown at a waterfall on the Lièvre, which starting from the Laurentian Mountains in the north runs into the eastward-flowing Ottawa about a hundred miles above the junction of the latter with the St Lawrence. The Lièvre had its place in Bernard's boyhood life too: swimming and rafting with Greg and Mark in the summer, Sunday sleigh rides on the frozen surface with their father in the winter (especially appreciated when the boys would otherwise have acolyte duties in the church at the tedious vesper service).

Of Bernard's home life, two items may be noted. One was the role of music; much later with evident feeling he would remember his mother at the piano, but when he visited home after eleven years with the Jesuits, and asked her to play, she declined: 'Oh, my fingers!'[4] The other item is strangely negative: reading does not seem to have been a family habit, at least in Bernard's early boyhood. His introduction to that came on one of the summer visits the Lonergan boys would make with their mother to a farm near Cornwall where her sister was married; one day when the six-year-old Bernard was finding time heavy on his hands, a cousin suggested that he read a book, so he started with *Treasure Island*.[5] Though this was apparently a new idea, the start was not really late by local standards, few Canadian boys of six being readers of more than comic strips.

There was one church in Buckingham (St Gregory Nazianzen) and one school (St Michael) for the Catholic population, but despite its name the town was predominantly French-speaking, so that in the English classrooms as many as three grades would be grouped in one room—a situation some might regard as chaotic, but one that Bernard found stimulating.[6] Credit for this must be given to the Brothers of Christian Instruction, and years later Bernard would pay tribute to the high standards of industry and achievement that they had set for him—in contrast to the Jesuits who, he would ruefully remark, taught him to loaf.

In 1918, at the age of thirteen, Bernard went as a boarder to Loyola College, a Jesuit school in Montreal. Various options had presented themselves, but he preferred Loyola to the others, judging it by circulars the school sent out. 'I was very impressed . . . that the boys wrote poetry . . . I had no hope of doing that myself, of course.'[7] Whether or not he wrote poetry he had a meteoric career at Loyola, skipping through preparatory, special Latin, second and third years of high school, all in one year. In fourth high, and through freshman and sophomore years of college, he kept to the normal pace, though he lost much of fourth high due to a very serious illness (a mastoid operation)—he received Extreme Unction, as it was then called, at the age of fifteen, the first in what would be a series of anointings during his life.

It is hard to get a steady picture of Bernard's view of the Jesuits in these early years, but he seems to have begun a lifelong symbiosis that, exaggerating considerably but making a valid point, I would call a love–hate relationship. He was happy at Loyola: 'The Jesuits were the best-educated people I had met', he would long afterwards say of his youthful experience. And apparently they helped set him on the way to his lifelong pursuit of understanding: 'I had some idea of it going through Loyola. I acquired great respect for intelligence.'[8] Further, he had a high regard for some of his teachers; the Latin–English dictionary he bought in his first year (it had somehow travelled to a Native Reservation in northern Ontario but made its circuitous way to the Archives after his death) has, among other schoolboy inscriptions: 'the teacher was William X. Bryan, SJ. He

4

was a very fine man. L.D.S. [*Laus Deo semper*—Praise to God always]' In accord with this is the testimony of a letter to his religious superior when he had been twelve years a Jesuit (we shall see the letter in context later): 'I know more luminously than anything else that I have nothing I have not received, that I know nothing in philosophy that I have not received through the society [of Jesus]'.[9]

But there was an ambivalence in his attitudes that persisted through life, that complicated his strong Jesuit loyalty, and is worth putting on the table at once. Here is a forthright passage, from a letter to another superior, John L. Swain, written when he had been 24 years in the Order. The context is a plea for higher standards of education:

> I went to Loyola as a boy of 13 from a parish school in B'ham. At the parish school I always had to work my hardest. At Loyola my acquired habits did not survive my first year: by the mid-term exams I was in 3rd High; by the end of the year I was fully aware that the Jesuits did not know how to make one work, that working was unnecessary to pass exams, and that working was regarded by all my fellows as quite anti-social. For my remaining three years at Loyola I loafed and passed exams with honors: during my second term in fourth high I was absent for the whole term, went up without taking exams, and never felt the slightest handicap from missing half a year of the course . . .
>
> Now do not tell me I am exceptional. I have more than average ability, but not so much more that I did not have to work when confronted with the standards of the parish school in Buckingham or the University of London.[10]

There were sharp remarks in other parts of the letter which brought a rebuke, it seems, from Fr Swain, for three weeks later there is an apology from Lonergan. But he does not seem to have retracted his damning judgement on the intellectual standards of Jesuit schools— damning even when we grant a certain freedom to exaggerate in a private letter to a religious superior.

It is best to get these criticisms out into the open at an early stage in our study; it will give perspective not only to the rest of this chapter but to the whole book. For his extremely negative view of the state of Catholic education would characterize Lonergan throughout life and orient all his efforts; not to realize that is not to understand his work. It was not just Loyola that he criticized: his Jesuit juniorate, his philosophy and theology, his doctorate programme too—all come under the same biting censure. Nor did he restrict his criticism to his own religious Order: Catholic studies in general were found to be in a deplorable state. We shall see the other pieces in the pattern as they occur, but the pattern itself needs to be declared at once; few other factors were at once so determinative for his career and so much hidden from the general public in this remote context of his work.

RELIGIOUS VOCATION

As with Lonergan's views on his Jesuit and Catholic studies, so with the account of his religious vocation: it is hard to get a steady picture. As a boy in Buckingham he was already thinking of religious life, but after his serious illness in his last year of high school he had abandoned the idea, thinking he lacked the necessary health. Then a Loyola Jesuit raised the question again, and convinced Bernard that his health was not an issue. His final decision had nothing exciting about it: 'I went out to the Sault [Montreal novitiate of the Jesuits of French Canada] to make a retreat, an election, and I decided on the street-car on the way out'.[11] A humdrum event surely, though the immediate effect was to determine his home for the next four years as the Jesuit Novitiate at Guelph, Ontario.

Guelph was an early focal point for the Jesuits when they returned to Ontario in the 1800s after their suppression. Missionaries from upstate New York travelled through the province, especially its western area, opening parishes and building churches right to the American border at Windsor/Detroit. Guelph had been founded in the 1830s by John Galt (who gave his name, however, to a neighbouring town), and the Jesuits arrived in due course to found Our Lady's church, built on the model of the Cologne cathedral; it was still their parish in Bernard's time at Guelph, and became familiar to him through frequent participation in its religious services.

The Jesuit Novitiate began in 1913 when it was decided that English-speaking candidates should have their own house. Guelph seemed a natural choice, so a 600-acre farm was bought for the purpose a couple of miles north of the town. Here young Bernard arrived on 29 July 1922, to begin a new life that would be another major orienting factor in all he would write and say for the next 60 years.

GUELPH: NOVITIATE YEARS

One can convey a scene, a trait of character, a dramatic episode, in a vignette or short story; there does not seem to be any art-form except the novel for creating a life. But novelists have full access to the consciousness of their characters; a historian can only collect the scattered data and make surmises. We know in general that the early years of religious in the motherhouse, their Bethlehem, are a long and sometimes painful introduction to a whole new way of living. For Bernard at Guelph this meant two years of novitiate training, and two of juniorate study with a heavy dose of novitiate discipline still maintained. The novices' and juniors' diaries of those years (still extant at Guelph) give cryptic headings for a monotonous succession of trivial events, but for me who went the same route fourteen years later, it is easy to recreate from them the slow process by which Bernard was turned into a religious.

Among the categories of the daily order one has to list first the ascetical side: readings of course, in the life of Christ and the saints, the *Imitation of Christ*, the Jesuit legal and spiritual documents, that old faithful by Alphonsus Rodriguez (1532–1617), *The Practice of Perfection and Christian Virtues*. There were the instructions from the master of novices (for Bernard this was Fr Arthur McCaffrey, a New York Jesuit who later went to the Philippines and returned blind, health shattered from years in a concentration camp), 'exhortations' preached by various grave fathers in the community, and so on. There were penances, publication of faults— voluntarily admitted or pointed out by one's fellows in their over-flowing *agape*—and there was a lot of prayer ('one gets through one's daily heavy dose of prayer'[12]), the slowest of all slow practices to learn. Bernard would say late in life that an injustice, as he thought it to be, ten years after he entered the Jesuit Order, taught him to pray; but not yet with joy, for still later he would volunteer the remark on spiritual joy: 'After twenty-four years of aridity in the religious life, I moved into that happier state and have enjoyed it now for over thirty-one years'.[13]

There was class and study. Though the focus was not on this, teachers were designated for the novices (with little scruple about sending in substitute teachers, if the regular one was away preaching), and they had regular classes—in Latin and Greek, of course, but also in English, French, singing (no spectacular results here for Bernard), and even in callisthenics.

There were domestic works in two categories. House maintenance (sweeping, dusting, cleaning toilets, the ever-present pots and pans to wash in the kitchen) provided ordinary works, *manualia*; these could be assigned for a month (as was the kitchen 'trial'—assistant to the community cook), or be new each morning. But, as occasion demanded— and it demanded quite frequently, a novitiate being a prime case of cheap conscript labour—there were extraordinary works: bringing in the hay or oats, helping with the milking (I doubt if Bernard ever did that—competence was required in the more important jobs), pouring cement in barn or basement, picking berries, hunting lost cows, work on the turnips (an entry of wonderful frequency those two years—what did they do with all those turnips?), keeping watch over the newly planted corn to scare away the crows, and in December watch over the distant pastures to discourage those hunting for free Christmas trees.

Life was by no means all prayer, study, and work. The regular 'recreation', noon and evening, hardly counted as play: it was an exercise in fraternal charity, 'bands' of three being appointed for the compulsory outdoor walking (this explains the otherwise mystifying 'free bands' in the diary), and a certain amount of conversation in Latin and French being required in the evening recreation. But there were holidays with games (Bernard was a good athlete, and regularly took part): baseball, hockey, tennis, volleyball, swimming in season, the occasional picnic, and walks in the surrounding countryside, with its numerous backroads and lanes. A 'villa' a mile away on the banks of the Speed river was the spot for the compulsory holiday on Thursdays, and in June–July first the novices, and then the juniors, had two or three weeks of vacation there.

Young Bernard made no headlines in novitiate news. He never got the top post of admonitor, a kind of beadle appointed by the master, but he was substitute admonitor from time to time, and in this capacity wrote the diary. It gave no scope, however, for English composition, consisting mainly of filling in the Latin *de more* for a routine day. With the others he functioned as catechist (the novices taught the Catholic children in the schools or homes of the surrounding countryside), and took his turn in exercises of elocution and preaching. There were two categories of sermon, one a weekly exercise before fellow-novices, the other, more formidable, at the community meals; it was a custom that the scholastic novices should preach during the visitation of the provincial superior, two or three at dinner, two or three at supper, till the list was finished— provincials were iron men in those days.

Most personal of all for Bernard must have been his 'pilgrimage', when in May of his second year he set out with a companion, Horatio Phelan, to walk as their sealed instructions, opened each day, would instruct them—generally a day's walk to the next rectory or whatever house would receive the 'pilgrims'. Bernard and Horatio were sent to Buffalo, via Niagara, setting out on 19 May, returning on 1 June, in good spirits, though Bernard had a cold (in fact the diary twice records him as sick for extended periods).

What did it all mean? What did it add to the piety of the Lonergan home and family? What did it do for the next 60 years of Bernard's life? All this is doubly a question, since the religious world of his elderly years was so different from that of his youth. But part of the answer is clear enough: it provided a solid basis for the kind of ascetical life his work would demand of him through long years of study and writing. Moreover, it entered his work to structure an intrinsic element of his thinking: the notion of self-transcendence. I do not think we really grasp the force of this key notion without reference to these formative years in which his own character was being transformed and developed. There is a picture of him at his desk in the Gregorian University, taken somewhere around 1960 when he was at the height of his powers, thin, ascetic, in cassock, with pen and paper, concentrated on his work—it represents the active part of his life and it was that kind of life for which his noviceship did much to prepare him.[14]

GUELPH: JUNIORATE YEARS

His two juniorate years were not so different in terms of house discipline: he would move from one part of the building to another (novices and juniors were kept segregated from one another by an 'iron curtain' of discipline), with the same house routine and a similarly strict ordering of the day (periods of study, of class, of prayer, of recreation, with occasional work—much reduced for juniors—on the farm). The focus, however, was sharply on study, with a strong stress on Latin, Greek, and English, and bits of time found for French, memory-work, sermon-writing, and—very important for Bernard—mathematics.

The juniorate diaries, like others, record special events in more detail, but the routine in brief headings, so they tell us only the *kind* of work the students did, and there is only casual mention of the authors studied: of Cicero, Virgil, Horace, Livy, and Tacitus (one of Lonergan's favourites[15]), of Plato and Demosthenes, of Homer,

Sophocles, and Euripides, of Kleutgen, of Shakespeare, Wordsworth, Coleridge, Francis Thompson. The inadequacy of the list is seen in the absence of Newman's name, though it was *de rigueur* to have him on a Catholic curriculum.[16] Again, there is mention of a memory examination at the end of a semester: 200 lines of Horace, and Wordsworth's *Ode on Intimations of Immortality*, but no mention of what was probably a daily dose of memory work.

In Bernard's first year two competent teachers had been assigned to the juniors: Fr Joseph Bergin for Latin (he was also the rector and prefect of studies), Mr Francis Smith (just through his philosophy studies) for Greek and English. Bernard was happy with them and his strictures on his juniorate teachers (we shall see them presently) do not apply till his second year. By that time he had his own teaching load: mathematics to a class of fellow-juniors, Latin and Greek to the novices. Moreover, he was appointed beadle of the juniors (counterpart to admonitor of the novices), and wrote the diary in that capacity from 21 July 1925 till he was relieved of the beadle's job on 12 February 1926. He was not an especially good diarist, and his handwriting at that time was atrocious, but allowance must be made for the extraordinarily busy year he had: studying, teaching, running the beadle's office, extra-curricular activities.

These latter were more extensive than one might expect. Lonergan took his turn at debates, elocution and the like. His first debate had to do with Catholic periodicals, it seems; other breathtaking topics 'resolved': that it is easier to begin the rudiments of Greek through Homer than through Attic prose; that the execution of Mary, Queen of Scots, was just; that Galileo was justly condemned; that the state should own and run the railroads. There were debates in French: resolved that the study of Latin is more help than the study of any other language, even for those who make a career in business; that Prohibition is more pernicious in its effects than the saloon. Elocution was a weekly exercise, but there were also 'sermons preached on various occasions'; for example, Lonergan preached before the community on the feast of St John Chrysostom, 26 January 1926—in Greek, and at dinner, not the best forum and procedure if we would convert anyone. The diary also records a playlet at Christmas of the previous year, *The Little Blasphemer*, where he had the part of 'Ephraim, Blind son of Cheops'.

It was a small self-contained world that is revealed in the diaries. The letters Lonergan wrote during his juniorate years to his friend, Henry Smeaton, do not change the picture.[17] They are full of the trivia that make up so large a part of a young Jesuit's life (or any-one's life, for that matter): a new rector, the arrival of his brother Gregory at Guelph, ministry at the nearby prison, a trip 90 miles north to Martyrs' Shrine. When they would rise above the trivial to generalities, they become stilted in style and somewhat trite in language.

But stone walls do not a prison make, nor need a self-contained world be small in the scope of its studies. The classics are classics, as much at Guelph as at Oxford; the ascetic life can flourish in the desert; the objectives of an international religious Order lead far beyond the observance of minute rules of daily routine. The juvenile style of the letters conceals an underlying transformation that would deeply affect his character and future work.

On the classics in particular and their role in education, I remem-ber an evaluation he gave us fifteen years later when, fresh from our own juniorate studies, we sat at his feet one summer day and asked him to tell us (guru-style, we would say now) what the value of the Greek and Latin classics was. The response was forthright: 'The work of translation takes you behind words to ideas'. But would not translation of modern languages do the same and be far more practi-cal? 'No, it's too easy in them to go from word to word and not get behind the words; you are forced back to the ideas when you trans-late the Latin and Greek classics.' I do not remember where the conversation went from there; I suppose that 30 years later he would talk of different grammatical structures, different stages of mean-ing, different levels of culture, and that there was something of this in 1941, but if so it apparently had little meaning for me, and did not stay in my memory.

Still, there are his later strictures on the level of his juniorate studies. The already quoted letter of 1946 goes on to say: 'In the juniorate I spent most of my study periods at private reading, cover-ing large tracts of the classics earnestly and with about 10% of the profit I could have had, had there been a teacher in the place'.[18] He voices a similar criticism of his juniorate English, this time in com-parison with Heythrop standards: 'I read Thackeray and kept a list of all the words, to know the meaning well enough to use them myself . . . I improved my vocabulary tremendously. But I went to England for philosophy, and all the lads there were talking that way.'[19]

What are we to make of this? I daresay the criticism is valid viewed as a whole, *in globo*, but, in the spirit of Newman's 'true way of learning', I would purge it of exaggerations. His '10% of the

11

profit' is obviously not to be taken literally. On the other hand, his estimate of the relative situations in Canada, England, and the Continent (we shall see this presently) was probably right on target for that time. And his being so largely self-taught was the beginning of a pattern that would continue into his doctorate work and beyond; indeed, I regard it as illuminating much of his career and the highly individual character of his thinking.

THE HEYTHROP YEARS: 1926–1930

The Jesuit province of English Canada had no house of philosophy studies in 1926—fortunately enough, for then their young men had to be sent out of province for this stage of formation, could experience other nations and other ways of life, and overcome in some degree the narrowness in regard to peoples and cultures which was as real a drawback at Guelph as any found in the programme of studies.

Heythrop Hall, located a few miles to the northwest of Oxford, had just been taken over by the Jesuits of England and, with the addition of two wings (one for philosophers 'based upon the old stabling accommodation of Mr. Brassey's famous Hunting Seat',[20] one for theologians), been turned into Heythrop College the very year that Bernard arrived there for philosophy studies.

The college opened with a community of 191: 84 to study theology, of whom seven were fellow-Canadians (among them Bernard's juniorate teacher, Francis Smith), 65 to study philosophy, of whom ten were Canadians; there were five in special studies, seventeen brothers, the rest were priests: professors and staff.

The philosophy beadle's diary records the minutiae of everyday life, in the style that was familiar to the 'colonials' from Canada, if the content would sometimes puzzle them: for example, the offices listed there of 'Fisherman . . . Astronomer . . . Weather-Prophet'. 'Postman' and 'Postmaster' were distinguished. 'Holy Water' required no less than three appointees, a reminder of the time when the entrance to every room had a holy-water font to be periodically refilled. Lonergan's name appears from time to time: his arrival on 14 September (coincidentally, with Fr Whiteside, who became one of his favourite professors), his refectory sermon on 16 February 1927 (we are not told whether this was his controversial one on Acts 28:26, 'You will hear and hear but not understand'[21]), his 'tones' (elocution exercise) on 13 March, his 'offices' (one of the class beadles in his second year), his lectures before the Philosophical and Literary Society (of which more later), his first-year examination scheduled for 11 July, and so on—the same literary genre we have already seen at Guelph.

Still, despite the familiar routine of daily class and prayer and community life, it was a new world for the Canadians. Lonergan, of course, was storing up experience for eventual insights; over 30 years later he would refer to the social strata of England to illustrate his ideas on the brands of common sense; 'The notion of specializations of common sense makes it clear how there can be complete incomprehension between people where classes become stratified'.[22] But he took to the English way, developing a lasting affection for English authors (G. K. Chesterton and Lewis Carroll were notable examples), even learning to appreciate the skills of cricket.

The prefect of studies in philosophy (as well as professor of natural theology, cosmology, and metaphysics) was Fr Joseph Bolland, the one who said on Bernard's confessing his nominalism, 'No one remains a nominalist very long'.[23] As listed that first year, Fr Henry Irwin lectured on pedagogy, Fr Victor Moncel on psychology and the history of philosophy, Fr Charles O'Hara on mathematics, Fr Lewis Watt on ethics, and Fr Philip Whiteside on logic, epistemology and general metaphysics. All of these would figure to the end of Bernard's life in his writings, memories, or interviews.

If his four years at Guelph were decisive for the young Bernard's spiritual formation, his four years at Heythrop seem to have been equally decisive for the intellectual element in his vocation. Yet his evaluation of those years follows the pattern already seen: it is not simple. His professors were honest and able, but the philosophy was second-rate; this, however, seems not to have mattered much, since the main interest for the better students was their work toward a degree at the University of London: 'anyone . . . with any brains was getting a university degree; that was his main concern'. The concern had its financial side for the English Jesuit schools: teachers with a university degree meant government grants.[24] The Heythrop administration understood the situation, and provided tutors: 'classes on the Latin and Greek authors were regularly held by Fr. Harry Irwin and on mathematics by Fr. Charles O'Hara'.[25]

Lonergan entered into this way of life; instead of studying philosophy, 'I was busy preparing exams at London'.[26] His four subjects at the university were Greek, Latin, French and mathematics. He would have taken methodology, and wrote to his provincial superior with that in mind; the latter, Fr John Filion, replied, 'No, do classics'. Later on Lonergan was grateful, judging the method he created better than what London would have given him.[27]

The letter of 1946 that was so critical of his juniorate continues in the same vein on his philosophate: 'In my years of philosophy or theology I never bothered about the matter . . . until repetitions began; I spent my time at private study'.[28] But once again we have to add qualifications. There are two short letters from Heythrop to Henry Smeaton. The first, dated 11 December 1926, for all its staccato style, is important for his early impressions: 'Heythrop is all right. Philosophy ditto.' The other is dated 20 June [1927].[29] Here we find the following remark. 'I am afraid I must lapse into philosophy. I have been stung with that monomania now and then but I am little scholastic though as far as I know a good Catholic still. The theory of knowledge is what is going to interest me most of all.' He goes on to speak of his reading in Aristotle.[30]

The letter is useful, not only to confirm the memories of 50 years later, that he had an early interest in cognitional theory, but also to give Heythrop philosophy somewhat higher marks than do his memories in 1980.[31] A likely explanation is that Bernard had considerable interest in philosophy during his first year, but that later his studies at the University of London encouraged a critical attitude that in any case would have grown increasingly severe.

The content of Heythrop philosophy need not detain us long. 'The textbooks were German in origin and Suarezian in conviction.'[32] They would be the matter he had later to 'unlearn'. The content of Lonergan's own thinking is more to the point, and happily he recorded some of it in the *Blandyke Papers* of January and March of 1928, and again in February and at Easter of 1929.

His very first article was called 'The form of mathematical inference'.[33] This is not the one that appeared in *Thought* fifteen years later as 'The form of inference',[34] but a quite distinct treatment of the act that would become famous as 'insight into phantasm'. He does not call it by that name; he probably does not realize the significance of his discovery; in fact, he attributes the act of insight to the Thomist *vis cogitativa* (he does not seem to have read Thomas at this time); but recognition of the act is unmistakable in his procedure and his language.

His procedure, so familiar from later lectures, is to study one of Euclid's proofs: in this case the proof that, when the base of a triangle is produced, the external angle thus formed is equal to the sum of the two interior opposite angles. Lonergan draws a line in the external angle parallel to the opposite side of the triangle, and asks how we know this line divides the external angle. One view is that the figure is only a help, that thought is concerned with triangularity as such ('triangularitate', in his odd English word, p. 133). It is easy to recognize here the archenemy of twenty years later: conceptualism. Lonergan rejects this view, arguing that Euclid dealt with the figure in the actual diagram. But if we insist on the particular figure, how do we know the proof applies to all triangles? Here Lonergan invites us to the exercise of a 'kinetic generic image' in which we swing the line through the whole exterior angle till it reaches coincidence with the near side of the triangle. 'Every instant we see a different triangle and in the infinity of triangles' the line 'is always a transversal of parallels' (p. 134). The problem from Euclid, occurring both here and in the first *verbum* article of 1946, securely ties the activity of the earlier paper to the later insight into phantasm.

His language confirms this. He begins by distinguishing 'two kinds of inference, one sensible the other conceptual' (p. 127), and it is easy to relate the second kind to conceptualism and the first to insight into phantasm—the terms of 1946. Sensible inference, despite the awkward name, is a matter of getting the idea through the image; it depends, he keeps saying, on 'visualization' (pp. 130, 132, 134, 137). Again, there is 'a directly and intuitively appre- hended relation' (p. 128), an apprehension 'in virtue of a generic image' (p. 129), what he at one point calls 'an intuition of the vis cogitativa' (p. 131; see also p. 129). Coming to the question whether our proof is valid for every triangle, Lonergan says, 'Visualize this triangle' (p. 134). Then in the kinetic generic *image* mentioned above we see at every instant a different triangle. At the end Lonergan draws his modest conclusion: 'the diagram is more important than . . . is ordinarily believed' (pp. 134-5).

I have elsewhere nominated that remark for the philosophical understatement of the century. Even toward the end of his life Lonergan will recall the advice of Charles O'Hara, his mathematics tutor: 'flag the diagram. Draw a diagram; mark all the values you know on it. You should be able then to see an equation or two equations—whatever you need—and get the solution. Don't learn the trigonometrical formula by heart; just flag the diagram and read off the formula.'[35] A final point to remark in this extraordinary paper of 1928 is its hint of a second level of intellectual operations: 'I do not think Cardinal Newman's illative sense is specifically the same as these concrete inferences but that question requires separate treatment' (pp. 136-7).

The 'separate treatment' would follow a year later, but meanwhile

Lonergan contributed an article on 'The syllogism'.[36] This is a paper he had given before the Philosophical and Literary Society, and would some years later revise and publish in *Thought*. It probably represents an interest of his first year of philosophy (we remember that the professor spent a good deal of the year on logic, and gave short shrift to epistemology[37]). But it gives clear signs of a mind that was already transcending logic toward the intellectualist position of the *verbum* articles. On the argument that A is greater than C, if A is greater than B and B is greater than C: 'it would seem that the mind, in virtue of a perceptual scheme or a visualization correlates A and C and draws a conclusion parallel to the intuition of the a priori axiom' (pp. 38–9; and three times in pp. 45–7 Lonergan refers to visualization or a perceptual scheme). Similarly, he defends the meaning of the predicate as denoting an attribute, against those who would substitute a class of objects to which the attribute belongs—once more his intellectualist rejection of conceptualism. The published form of the paper will make that clear when it sets this little excursus in the pattern of Lonergan's life: 'our conclusion has to do with the nature of the human mind'; 'we . . . have aimed at taking a first step in working out an empirical theory of human understanding and knowledge'.[38]

More important is Lonergan's third contribution,[39] the 'separate treatment' called for in his first article, for it is largely a study of Newman's illative sense, and thus the forerunner of his own theory of rational consciousness; there is more than a hint also of the next step, rational self-consciousness, so we have the third and fourth levels of the later intentional structure. The article begins with the difference between a scientific investigation and a judgement. In the former, 'truth is not only known but also known to be known' (p. 195). The tactic of the paper is determined by this: 'if true judgment may be consciously true, then science ceases to be the one measure for certitude' (ibid.). Now this is the contention of Newman in his *Grammar of Assent* (1870), and the principle of the reflex knowledge in question is the illative sense. One can see here the reflective element of the level of judgement, though it is far from being worked out as well as it will be in the second *verbum* article. There is discussion of Newman's true way of learning (pp. 201–2), of the distinction of real and notional apprehension (pp. 205–9), of the role of wisdom and of growth in moral character in relation to judgement (pp. 210–16). His summary of the central argument sets against science and the syllogistic method the 'alternative criterion' of 'the mind itself' which is 'far higher, wider, more certain, subtler, than logical inference' (p. 209).[40]

Not everything in these early papers will retain its importance in later cognitional theory, but the links are plain. They are especially plain for insight into phantasm, where the path leads directly from 'The form of mathematical inference' to the *verbum* articles of 1946–49. The role of wisdom and the conditions for wisdom are not so different in 'True judgment and science' from what we see in those articles. The distinction between concrete inference and scientific investigation forecasts *Insight*'s contrast of concrete judgements of fact with those of scientific probability. Logic is already reduced to its subordinate role and, most important of all, the primacy is given to the alternative criterion of 'the mind itself'.

REGENCY

The Jesuit pattern of formation, then as now, introduced a period called regency between philosophical and theological studies, in which the young Jesuit was expected to teach, to coach athletic teams, to oversee student publications, to be prefect of dormitories, and in general to make himself useful to the school or college in question. For Bernard Lonergan this meant three years at Loyola College, Montreal.

Data are scarce on the contribution of these years to his formation, and to the context of his later writings. It is clear, however, that they did have a role in the integral story. For one thing he formed friendships that would be lifelong. For another, there was apparently a crisis at this time in his religious vocation; we have only vague accounts of this from his contemporaries, but it seems that the general difficulties of regency, compounded by an unhappy relationship to his superior and by the departure from the Order of two friends, was the occasion for him to rethink his vocation and commit himself anew to the life he had chosen eleven years earlier.[41] I have noted that an injustice at this time, as he saw it, taught him to pray; the injustice was the imposition of a fourth year of regency—his year at the University of London counted for one—a rather severe rebuke in the Jesuit scheme of things. But the snub of the fourth year was only one item in a pattern: 'I had regarded myself as one condemned to sacrifice his real interests and, in general, to be suspected and to get into trouble for things I could not help and could not explain'.[42]

As for the intellectual side of his regency, he taught a variety of courses (it was not yet the era of specialization—a competent Jesuit should be able to teach anything!), combining this with less intellectually demanding duties: 'My first year . . . I taught Latin, Greek, French and English and had the College debating society, the newsletter and the annual review'.[43] The next year he taught calculus and analytic geometry. He also taught, perhaps the same year, a course in mechanics—a fact that sheds an interesting light on the familiarity *Insight* shows with that branch of knowledge.[44] But it is difficult to determine in general whether his teaching advanced his mental formation a great deal. It was an era in which the emphasis in Catholic education was on the word 'Catholic'. His views in the 1946 letter on the state of Catholic studies in England, and by implication those of France, he would and did apply *a fortiori* to the Canadian situation:

> The English Jesuits make no bones about admitting that academically their schools cannot compete with such places as Eton or Harrow . . . And their patrons, if good Catholics, accept the situation. As M. Gilson is reported to have remarked recently: I gave my children a Catholic education, but it was a great sacrifice.[45]

Regency was not, however, a matter of three years in an intellectual desert. There was the challenge of students whom he regarded as outstanding.[46] And there were hidden advances of which we have a hint in the vague remark: 'despite the variety of my duties [I] was able to do some reading'. We cannot say how extensive this reading was, but the two samples he mentions would be quite influential in later life. 'Christopher Dawson's *The Age of the Gods* introduced me to the anthropological notion of culture and so began the correction of my hitherto normative or classicist notion.' Another book which 'greatly influenced' him at this time, ending his nominalism, was J.A. Stewart's *Plato's Doctrine of Ideas*:

> From Stewart I learned that Plato was a methodologist, that his ideas were what the scientist seeks to discover . . . My apprehension, at that time, was not that precise. It was something vaguer that made me devote my free time to reading Plato's early dialogues . . . then moving on to Augustine's early dialogues.[47]

There was even a bit of writing during regency, for he contributed two short pieces to *The Loyola Review*: an article on his beloved Chesterton (there was a rewrite of this ten years later), and one on the new college chapel. The latter is true to his developing form in its easy passage from the concrete details of architecture to the sweep of world history, but it is quite unexpected in its mastery of the architecture itself.[48] Perhaps also we should credit his regency period with an essay the 1935 letter speaks of: 'I read St Augustine's earlier works during the summer before theology and found him to be psychologically exact. I then put together a 25,000 word essay upon the act of faith.'[49]

THEOLOGY IN ROME

We come to the period that I consider as far and away the most significant for his future career of Lonergan's young life: his four years in Rome for the study of theology. The dark clouds of his regency years had vanished, his hope of an academic career been clarified and given substance, and so he mapped out in considerable detail his ideas for the integral renewal of Catholic thought. Texts, though still only in draft, are emerging now from the context; formation is yielding its first-fruits. The documentation is meagre but extremely precious: some newsy letters to Henry Smeaton in his first year, 1933–34; some memories of those years in later interviews; a review published in the *Gregorianum*, the university journal; but most precious of all are a letter to his provincial superior, Henry Keane, on 22 January 1935, and several surviving sheaves of his actual efforts to rethink Catholic doctrine—the sheaves of 'File 713' that we will presently study.

Lonergan did not begin his theology studies in Rome; the status changes of 1933 (traditionally announced on 31 July) sent him to the Collège de l'Immaculée-Conception in Montreal (where incidentally he caught up with his old friend, Henry Smeaton, now ordained and beginning fourth-year theology). But in November his provincial superior, Fr William Hingston, dispatched him to do theological studies with other Canadian Jesuits in Rome.

Just over a year later (January 1935) he provides some details of this event in the already much quoted letter to Henry Keane, his new provincial.[50] 'At this juncture Fr Hingston paid a flying visit to the Immaculate where I had begun my theology. I was to go to Rome. I was to do a biennium in philosophy. He put the question, Was I orthodox? I told him I was but also that I thought a lot' (p. 3). Fr Hingston was apparently satisfied with this profession of faith; at any rate, his decision remained to send Lonergan to Rome.

It was a decision that not merely determined an intellectual career for Lonergan, but buoyed him up immensely when he had developed a kind of fatalistic resignation to disappointment: he was 'completely elated at the prospect of going to Rome'. We recall his remark, 'I had regarded myself as one condemned to sacrifice his real interests and, in general, to be suspected and to get into trouble for things I could not help and could not explain'. And so he could now write 'Here was a magnificent vote of confidence which . . . after years of painful introversion . . . was consolation indeed' (pp. 3–4). His elation had to do with what he regarded as a vindication and a promise of a desired career. Whether it included hopes for the theology he might be taught at the Gregorian University is not stated; if it did, the hopes (like his work habits when he went as a boy to Loyola) would not long survive.[51] But in the beginning at least he found life in Rome highly agreeable; the buoyancy with which he received his assignment appears in his letters to Keane and Smeaton, with regard to the city, the university, the life style itself, as well as his personal religious life and academic hopes.

The 1935 letter to Henry Keane, with Lonergan now in his second year in Rome, starts with two pages dealing with matters of religious discipline. For example he asks for renewal of his smoking permission, apologizing for the cost. Likewise of his permission to read books on the Index of Prohibited Books, in which context it emerges that he was to do doctorate studies in epistemology (p. 1). Again, we learn something of the very modest library he is collecting: 'a number of texts from the Oxford plain Classics (4 Plato, 2 Aristotle, Thucydides, Tacitus, Aeschylus), Pindar with trans., translated selections of Plotinus', with dictionaries, manuals, and others (p. 2).[52]

But the real source under the heading of life in Rome is his correspondence with Henry Smeaton.[53] His Christmas card to Henry is favourable on almost every count: 'Zapelena [professor of ecclesiology] a master. Canonisation an event to take you off your feet [he was there for that of St Bernadette Soubirous] . . . Am still breathless with enthusiasm for Rome . . . Meals excellent . . . Italians the soul of naturalness.' But there is a hint of the criticism to come: 'Study a minor detail here—about $1\frac{1}{2}$ hours on class days'.

A long letter next May shows him still enthralled with the city:

I do not know if I have conveyed to you yet any of that 'timelessness' that characterises life in the 'eternal' city. It is borne in upon me most of all when in the longer walks we go to the

Borghese—a villa with magnificent gardens open to the public—
and seated on a bench watch the children frolic, and people pass,
and punts row leisurely about the lake, and the stone tritons with
ever-distended cheeks spurt columns of water high into the air
(p. 4).

I can sit for an hour under the shade of the holm oaks and let
serenity creep in upon me through the gateway of lethargy
(p. 5).

But criticism is sharpening:

on the whole it is difficult to do as the Romans do with the new
constitution of studies. Maurice Baring in one of his novels
makes a character say to another who was planning to study in
Rome 'Who ever heard of anyone getting any work done in
Rome!' . . . Certainly, whoever . . . drew up our daily routine
made no provision for private study. The whole morning at
lectures on an empty stomach so that you cannot but eat a
soporific dinner and so be out of action till the next lecture at
4 p.m. (pp. 5–6).

It is May and so examination time approaches: 'the matter for the
exams was allotted in pressed-down over-flowing measure' (p. 1).
'The third exam we have might be called the pure theory of Canon
Law. It's handed out by a too well-informed Spaniard . . . and has
a most catholic taste in the questions it treats' (p. 8). But he
speaks highly of the man teaching the inspiration of the scriptures
[Sebastien Tromp] and in general is not too severe on his professors
(pp. 8–9).
   Some discussion of assignments among the Canadian Jesuits led
Lonergan to his views on what the home province needed, and in
particular to a working relationship he would like to establish with
Smeaton:

I think the parallel is obvious. You are a man that certainly will
be before the public and you will be before the public not on
philosophic issues—the public does not think that deeply—but
upon scriptural questions. Moreover, if I am to be an apologist,
I shall certainly want someone on whom I can call . . . in that
line. Again, I don't admit without qualification the view that this
generation is to be sacrificed to routine work for the sake of the

21

next. There has to be a flash in the pan to breathe life into things, now, to make the project of a U [university] seem real—not merely to our Provincial who sees but also to the Province which does not (p. 12).

This brings us back to our main topic, the context for Lonergan's academic career and for his ideas on the renewal of Catholic studies. The letter of January 1935 to Henry Keane[54] relates some of the history of his assignment to teach philosophy; let us recap what we have seen and add a few details: Lonergan's question to Fr Bolland on leaving Heythrop, whether to work on mathematics or classics; Bolland's suggestion of philosophy or theology; Lonergan's objection of his nominalism, 'while admitting philosophy to be my fine frenzy' (p. 3)—the objection that Bolland rather pooh-poohed. Lonergan then reports his study of Plato during regency, of Augustine in the summer before theology, and of turning to Thomas Aquinas: 'I then went on to study the Summa at first hand and began to suspect that St Thomas was not nearly as bad as he is painted'.

Lonergan has not yet entered his period of apprenticeship to Thomas; it is rather criticism of the Thomists than enthusiasm for Thomas that characterizes the present letter:

The current interpretation . . . is a consistent misinterpretation . . . what the current Thomists call intellectual knowledge is really sense knowledge. . . . I can work out a luminous and unmistakeable meaning to intellectus agens et possibilis, abstractio, conversion to phantasm, intellect knowing only the universal, illumination of phantasm, etc. etc. . . . At the same time I can deduce the Thomist metaphysic: universal individuated by matter; real distinction of essence and existence; the whole theory of act and potency (p. 4).

Now immediately to the point:

I can put together a Thomistic metaphysic of history that will throw Hegel and Marx, despite the enormity of their influence on this very account, into the shade. I have a draft of this already written as I have of everything else. It takes the 'objective and inevitable laws' of economics, of psychology (environment, tradition) and of progress (material, intellectual; automatic up to a point, then either deliberate and planned or the end of a

22

civilisation) to find the higher synthesis of these laws in the mystical body (p. 5).

There follows some account of this history, some explanation of the decadence of philosophy after Thomas, some account of what was going on in modern philosophy. Lonergan admits his limited acquaintance with the latter, gained only through 'such summaries as history of philosophy gives and occasional studies of particular authors'. But he feels he knows something about it and refers to the good opinion held of him by Fr Keeler, professor of the history of philosophy at the Gregorian University. He asserts also that 'Louvain substantially agrees with me' (p. 6; earlier, p. 4, he had been more explicit on Maréchal).

What are we to make of this extraordinary letter and these extraordinary claims? The answer would have to depend on what Lonergan had already produced, and the evaluation of that, in the absence of documentation, depends to some extent on the fulfilment of the next 45 years. Sharper critics will call the letter brash; milder ones, however, will remember that we are not studying a manifesto to the public, but a very private self-manifestation of a religious to his superior, in which he opens his mind and heart on where he is and what he hopes to do. Indeed, one does not escape a certain feeling of guilt in prying into such an open manifestation of soul. Happily, another part of the letter somewhat softens the features his critical remarks would draw; it was quoted earlier but is worth repeating now in fuller context:

> Naturally I think this is my work but I know more luminously than anything else that I have nothing I have not received, that I know nothing in philosophy that I have not received through the society. I do not say I am a Stoic or that I don't care . . . I do care enormously about the good of the church but I also know that what I do not do through obedience will be done better by some one else. God can raise up from stones children to Abraham. To produce philosophers is simply a matter in the natural order (p. 8).

What the letter in effect announces, and what File 713 will exemplify, is a broadening in the horizons of his thinking and interests. The study of cognitional theory retains its early attraction, and philosophy is still his 'fine frenzy', but philosophy had come to mean something other than the meaning currently given it, and cognitional theory would be subordinate for a time to his interest in history. A letter in the summer preceding his doctoral studies has this to say:[55]

As philosophy of history is as yet not recognised as the essential branch of philosophy that it is, I hardly expect to have it assigned me as my subject during the biennium. I wish to ask your approval for maintaining my interest in it, profiting by such opportunities as may crop up, and in general devoting to it such time as I prudently judge can be spared (p. 2).

This agrees with the papers of File 713, some of them written the previous few years, some of them perhaps occupying him this very summer of 1938. They show his interests to lie in the field of culture, philosophy of history, human sciences such as sociology, politico-economic questions, and the like. Cognitional theory was never far from the centre, but these papers of 1934 to 1938 have another focus.

'FILE 713—HISTORY'

Lonergan had kept until his death a manila folder marked 'History' and numbered 713 in the organization of his papers. It contains notes on Toynbee's *A Study of History*, but these are later, dating from his reading of Toynbee in the early 1940s. Our present interest is rather in a collection of earlier papers: eight items of varying length (from one to 36 pages), that appear from internal evidence to have been written while Pius XI was Pope, before the war broke out, and before Lonergan began his doctoral studies in the fall of 1938. One of them happens to be dated very precisely 'Dominica in Albis 1935' (28 April that year), the others belong to the same phase of his development, so the set of eight in all probability belong to the years 1934 to 1938. There is a great deal of repetition in these papers—evidently Lonergan was working and reworking his ideas—so we can get a sufficiently accurate idea of his thinking at this time by selecting and examining three of them.[56]

I begin with the one that is dated, *Pantôn Anakephalaiôsis* (28 April 1935). It is rather formally produced, and so much a finished essay that Lonergan showed it to a critic, and kept the critic's comments in his file.[57] A cascade of subtitles gives more than a hint of what Lonergan is about: *A Theory of Human Solidarity. A*

24

Metaphysic for the Interpretation of St Paul. A Theology for the Social Order, Catholic Action, And the Kingship of Christ, in incipient outline. The title is based on Ephesians 1:10, but a motto at the top of the title-page is from the *Summa Theologiae* of Thomas Aquinas, and speaks of our intellect as advancing from potency to act, through the medium of an incomplete act in which things are known indistinctly and confusedly. Lonergan, it seems, had learned from Thomas the idea of development of human intelligence before he discovered in Thomas the act itself of intelligence, insight into phantasm.

A key notion of the paper is human solidarity across time; there are ramifications of the notion, as when Lonergan discusses our relationship to Adam and to Christ, takes up questions of the one and the many, of sin and grace, examines the course of history, and so on. The field is that of sociology rather than cognitional theory or metaphysics; indeed at one point (p. 18), commenting on the instruction of Pius XI that candidates for the priesthood should undertake an 'intense study of social matters', Lonergan writes: 'This command has not yet been put into effect, nor can it be till there is a Summa Sociologica'. But cognitional theory and metaphysics do enter, as the six section-titles indicate: (1) Liberty as a disjunctive determination. (2) The historical determination of intellect. (3) The unity of human operation. (4) The synthesis of human operation. (5) The unity of man in the ontological ground of his being. (6) *Pantôn Anakephalaiôsis* (this last section is about half the essay).

Cognitional theory and metaphysics have, then, been worked out in some detail, at least to the extent needed for his study, but they are not the focus of his attention. History, on the contrary, is so interwoven with his argument that it emerges quite naturally as the main topic in the later papers and explains the title Lonergan gave this file. I speak of 'later' papers on the evidence of his own autobiographical remarks in 1973: 'It was about 1937–38 that I became interested in a theoretical analysis of history. I worked out an analysis on the model of a threefold approximation . . .'—and Lonergan went on to illustrate the model by the laws of planetary motion.[58] It does seem that the series of papers announcing history as the theme, and using this same model, should belong to the end of this period and so to the years 1937–38.[59]

We can, however, distinguish two approaches in the papers on history, one a more analytic study of the elements in a theory, the other more an application of the analysis to the concrete course of history. A good representative of the first is the essay called simply *Analytic Concept of History*, perhaps the latest in the set of eight.[60] I note the eight subtitles in its table of contents: (1) Analytic concepts. (2) History. (3) The Dialectic. (4) The Three Categories. (5) The Ideal Line of History. (6) Decline. (7) Renaissance. (8) The Multiple Dialectic. Numbers 5, 6 and 7, more familiar to readers of *Method in Theology* as progress, decline and redemption, spell out singly the three categories of number 4, with Newton's first law of motion serving as model for the ideal line.

The other approach is found in the perhaps earlier paper, *Philosophy of History*.[61] It is not self-contained but paginated 95–130, with little indication of what pages 1–94 held.[62] The first few pages (95–102) give the idea of a philosophy of history, and would, if our chronology is correct, anticipate the essays that deal expressly with analysis of history; they conclude (pp. 101–2) with a distinction 'between two phases in human progress: the automatic stage in which there is a constant succession of brilliant flowerings and ultimate failures; the philosophic stage in which the historical expansion of humanity has its ultimate control in a sound philosophy that not only is sound but also is able to guide the expansion effectively'. This gives four periods in the actual course of human events: A. The world prior to the discovery of philosophy, that is, up to Socrates, Plato and Aristotle. B. The failure of philosophy to fulfil its social mission, that is, from Plato to the Dark Age. C. The automatic cultural expansion following upon the Dark Age and continuing up to the present. It has had sound philosophy but no social consciousness of the social necessity of philosophy. D. The future.

The rest of the essay (pp. 102–30) takes up these divisions one by one, though it is not clear whether 'the philosophic estimate of the future', Lonergan's fourth section, which begins on page 113, is still the theme from page 116 on. A sentence that shows his social interest is worth quoting (p. 117): 'We note in passing that the hope of the future lies in a philosophic presentation of the supernatural concept of social order'. Also, in view of his work long years after, the remark (p. 116), 'in every economic question the antiquated sovereignty of the state is the fundamental difficulty; this will sufficiently appear from our discussion of economics'.[63]

Even this sketchy account of File 713 will surprise students of Lonergan introduced to him through his cognitional theory and metaphysics. To read it and notice the continual references to current events[64] is so unexpected in one who seemed to begin his career with two historical studies of mediaeval thought, *gratia operans* and

26

the *verbum*, and continue it with studies of intentionality analysis and method, that one wonders what became of this work of Lonergan's youth, how he turned from what was so topical to what was so remote, and why he kept these papers all his life, if he had abandoned the direction he seemed to have taken in them. Or *did* he abandon it, did it endure as an underlying purpose, and can one find it all-pervasive in his later work? Was there a massive withdrawal in preparation for an equally massive return? In which case the question would become one of his overall strategy. Did he have such a strategy? Did he perhaps work haphazardly at what caught his momentary attention? The latter is so unlikely in one who had an absolute passion for planning his books and articles that it need hardly be considered. But is there a third possibility, between a 'planned' life and a rudderless one? We are left with many questions about his overall purpose, his tactics, and his particular decisions over the next ten years.

TERTIANSHIP: AMIENS, 1937–38

One period of his life (1937–38) remains to be noted before we turn to his eleven-year apprenticeship[65] to Thomas Aquinas: his year of tertianship, a short ten months but regularly a profound experience for Jesuits. The name derives from its being regarded as a third year of novitiate, with the influences of a novitiate operating at a deeper level and on the basis of several years of experience.

The province of French Jesuits called Champagne, which included houses and colleges at Boulogne, Colmar, Dijon, Lille, Metz, Nancy, Rheims, and other places, had also a house of tertianship in Amiens, with Fr Leon Aurel in the highly influential post of tertian-instructor. There were 23 tertians there in 1937–38, including one of Bernard's fellow-Canadians from Rome, and the English Jesuit, Paul Kennedy, who would himself become one of the more famous tertian-instructors of the next generation.[66]

We have no letters from tertianship itself, no writings drafted for publication, and, except possibly for some papers of File 713,[67] no ideas sketched out for the renewal of Catholic thought. But there is a kind of diary of his 30-day retreat, and there are memories of this year in the interviews. These sources, minimal though they be, shed some light on his personal life and its relation to his career.

From the diary we can confirm what we noticed, or surmised, about his novitiate: the fundamental orientation, affecting even his life of study, to the aims of his religious vocation. To illustrate this, we have only to read the analysis (pp. 30–1) of reasons for and against choosing, or volunteering for, a life on the missions of his Church. It comes as something of a shock, this 'possible' or maybe 'futurable', this what-might-have-been or what-would-have-been-if; we form a picture of a Bernard Lonergan snowshoeing around northern Ontario from one Indian reservation to another, or teaching Nepalese students in a Darjeeling high school, with all his writings remaining in the world of mere potency.

From the interviews we have his account in '*Insight* revisited' of going from Amiens to Paris for a week at the *Ecole sociale populaire* at Vanves. We have been accustomed to read this account for its impact on the young Lonergan's notion of obedience,[68] but with File 713 in mind we read it with new eyes: they listened to four talks a day from leaders of 'the *mouvements spécialisés* of Catholic Action then in full swing'. Catholic Action, we remember, occurs as a phrase in one of the subtitles of the 1935 essay, *Pantôn Anakephalaiôsis*. Further, although he had asked for and received permission to go at the end of tertianship (probably in July 1938) to *Action Populaire*, he did not take advantage of the granted permission but, as he wrote from Ireland in August: 'I . . . came directly here from tertianship because I felt I needed all the time I could get to put retreat notes "au point" '. He was busy preparing to give retreat talks to the Loretto Sisters of Wexford.

We have seen this letter from Ireland before: it is the one in which he expressed to his provincial superior his interest in philosophy of history: 'As philosophy of history is as yet not recognised as the essential branch of philosophy that it is, I hardly expect to have it assigned me as my subject during the biennium'.[69] In any case that question had become irrelevant, for letters were crisscrossing the Atlantic (extraordinary efficiency in the mails of those years though letters went by surface) to get him transferred from philosophy to theology.[70] The negotiations succeeded, he must have been informed of this in the late summer, and headed for Rome for the November opening of classes. It would mean a long interruption in his pursuit of the objectives of the 1930s.

I tried, as I began this long chapter, to justify its insertion on the ground that it is context for the life of thought which we know from Lonergan's writings. It supplies some elements of history that are unknown to most of his readers, though by that very fact it reveals also the need for a thorough biography of the type now being prepared by others.

As I justified its insertion by appeal to one of Lonergan's ideas, let me try to justify its length by appeal to another. His deep study of human development in chapter 15 of *Insight* speaks of a kind of reversal of roles as development unfolds, with the underlying materials playing a more important part in the early stages, but yielding place more and more to higher elements in later stages. On application of this principle, material details of place and time and circumstance need less study when we analyse, say, *Insight*, than when we analyse *Pantôn Anakephalaiôsis*. The reader may therefore hope for a more direct engagement with Lonergan's thought in the following chapters.

Notes

1   'Hermeneutics' (unpublished notes for a lecture during the Institute on Method in Theology [*De methodo theologiae*], Regis College, Willowdale, Toronto, 9–20 July 1962), p. 14.
2   Ibid.
3   For data on the Lonergan family, I rely, making minor corrections, on J. V. Rice, 'The Lonergans of Buckingham', *Compass: A Jesuit Journal* (*Special Issue Honouring Bernard Lonergan S. J. 1904–1984*; Spring 1985), pp. 4–5. For data on the mother's side, I rely on notes, provided by Cyril Morris, on John Harrison (1784–1832) and his descendants. For the whole period of Lonergan's youthful formation, I am much indebted to research notes provided by William Mathews.
4   P. Lambert, C. Tansey and C. Going (eds), *Caring about Meaning: Patterns in the Life of Bernard Lonergan* (Montreal, 1982), pp. 236–7; see also pp. 194–5. This book is 'an edited transcript of conversations with Bernard Lonergan on six afternoons: Monday to Friday, February 16–20, 1981, and Thursday, May 20, 1982' (p. vii). It contains a wealth of information, but we must note that Lonergan, in hospital when it was going to press and unable to examine it properly, later expressed reservations on several passages.
5   P. Lambert, 'Introduction', ibid., p. vii. But reading habits developed: William Mathews told me that when 'Aunt Minnie' (Josephine Lonergan's sister) joined the family, she brought with her a set of Dickens, which they would read, sitting round the fire. The two interests of music and reading remained late in life; asked in these same interviews whether music was his most permanent artistic interest, he replied, 'Yes, in a sense. But writing is art too, you know', and went on to speak of Evelyn Waugh (p. 195). He delighted in *The New Yorker* (to which a friend gave him a subscription in his later years), and it is not out of place to mention the fine prose that occurs in his own writing—the fruit of long study and exercise, though it seems to occur quite naturally.

6   *Caring*, p. 132: '. . . in the ungraded school you kept working. If . . . you had one teacher talking all day long, you just wasted your time.'

7   Ibid., pp. 133–4.

8   Ibid., pp. 135, 142.

9   B. Lonergan, letter to his provincial superior (Henry Keane), 22 January 1935, p. 8. This, and other letters quoted here, are to be found in the Archives of the Lonergan Research Institute, Toronto. The Latin–English dictionary is kept in the same Archives. Another Loyola teacher he mentions was Joseph Keating (*Caring*, p. 21), who introduced him to the phrase *quid sit*, but without apparently explaining it (*quid sit?*, what is it? and *an sit?*, is it so? are the two questions that later structure Lonergan's cognitional theory). Further evidence of his love for his religious Order: 'Quatercentenary', *Loyola College Review* 27 (1941), pp. 22–5.

10   B. Lonergan, letter to his provincial superior (John L. Swain), 5 May 1946. See also a memo sent to Swain in a follow-up, 24 May: 'In England they smile very tolerantly at colonial universities; in France and Germany they smile at English universities. But what is galling about this smiling is that it is completely and fully justified. . . . I know that I cannot produce the stuff that a European scholar would produce with half the labor I put in.'

11   *Caring*, pp. 131, 133, 136, 141. There was question first of his joining the Brothers who taught him in Buckingham, but Bernard's father opposed that (p. 131). He gave up his idea of a religious vocation after high school (p. 136), thinking he was 'liberated' by his serious illness (p. 141).

12   B. Lonergan, 'Existenz and aggiornamento' in *Collection*, ed. F. E. Crowe and R. M. Doran (2nd edn; *Collected Works of Bernard Lonergan* 4, Toronto, 1988), p. 231. This chapter was a lecture of September 1964.

13   B. Lonergan, letter of 16 August 1977, to Louis Roy, who has kindly provided a copy. I have lost my source for the remark on the 'injustice' that taught him to pray, but he meant his being given four years of regency instead of the usual three.

14   There is a piety in Lonergan that surfaces in a way unusual in theological writings—in such simple manifestations as speaking of 'our Lady', or of God's effort through Calvary to 'touch our hard hearts', or concluding a lecture by asking all to pray for the institute sponsoring the lecture, or—most remarkable—reminding readers at the end of *Insight* that success in their search for truth 'is principally the work of God'.

15   I owe to Fred Lawrence the detail that Tacitus was a main influence for Lonergan's Latin style, and that a Latin review he wrote in 1935 for *Gregorianum* (16, pp. 156–60—of L. W. Keeler, *The Problem of Error, from Plato to Kant*) was done in the style of Tacitus, but that Fr Eric Smith revised it to Ciceronian.

16   We learn from a chance remark years later that he read *The Present Position of Catholics* at Loyola and *The Idea of a University* in the juniorate (*Caring*, p. 15); presumably, his reading ranged more widely in Newman than these hints reveal.

17   There is a set of eleven missives from Lonergan to Henry Smeaton, varying in length from a postcard to a 12-page letter. Written between 1924 and 1934, they were kept by Fr Smeaton in a nomadic career (it took him through the battles of World War II) and found among his effects on his death in 1980. A passage in one of the letters suggests there was other correspondence; if so, it has been lost, as was Smeaton's side of the exchange.

18   B. Lonergan, letter to John L. Swain, 5 May 1946. This criticism does not apply to his first year; he told me (conversation in summer of 1965) that Fr Bergin, whom he had as Latin teacher, was 'very intelligent', and that Mr Smith, whom he had for Greek and English, was 'competent'. See also *Caring*, p. 135, on his early view of Jesuits as well-educated people: 'I didn't retain that notion very long, but to my fourth year in the Jesuits [second-year juniorate], I had no reason to doubt it'. Both Bergin and Smith had left the juniorate by that time.

19   *Caring*, p. 217. To evaluate the young Lonergan's programme of studies we need missing information on the integration or lack of it in his courses at Loyola, Guelph, and the University of London. It has happened that novices spent two years learning again the accidence of Greek and Latin that they already knew.

20   *Letters and Notices* (Newsletter of the English Jesuits) 40 (1925), p. 295; there is considerable information on Heythrop College in the pages of this journal. For a photocopy of pages from the diary of the Heythrop philosophers I am indebted to William Mathews.

21   *Caring*, pp. 6–7.

22   *Understanding and Being: The Halifax Lectures on* Insight, ed. Elizabeth A. Morelli and Mark D. Morelli (2nd edn; *Collected Works of Bernard Lonergan* 5, Toronto, 1990), p. 91. Some of the cultural differences he found: 'I went to England to study from 1926 to 1930, and I found that everything there moved about four times more slowly than in Canada. Then I went to Rome to study theology, and I discovered that there everything moved about four times more slowly than in England' (ibid.). On Canadian and European universities at the time see the passage quoted in note 10 above.

23   B. Lonergan, '*Insight* revisited' in *A Second Collection*, ed. W. Ryan and B. Tyrrell (London/Philadelphia, 1974/1975), p. 264.

24   *Caring*, p. 8. Lonergan is rather forthright at times on the Heythrop philosophy. They learned little of modern philosophy (p. 16). 'There was no enthusiasm for philosophy' (p. 47). 'I felt that there was absolutely no method to the philosophy I had been taught' (p. 10). Any ideas he picked up were 'mostly negative' (p. 47). His own attitude became correspondingly negative—for theology too: 'I had no interest in philosophy or theology' (ibid.); 'I certainly didn't work hard at philosophy or theology when I was a student' (p. 8). The Heythrop course started with the rejection of universal scepticism (p. 47)—certainly not an approach that would appeal to the author of *Insight*, for whom the question was not whether knowledge existed but what its nature was.

   Still, all this criticism has to be qualified, in regard to both Heythrop and his own interest in philosophy (see note 31 below).

31

25 B. Lonergan, '*Insight* revisited', p. 263. Lonergan often spoke of the role played by Fr O'Hara in his own understanding of mathematics (*Caring*, pp. 1, 2, 4, 9).

26 *Caring*, p. 47. This at least was the case from second year on (p. 16).

27 *Caring*, p. 10. See also p. 137: 'The only time I had an idea of what I'd like to study, I wanted to do methodology. Now I'm glad they wouldn't let me.'

28 B. Lonergan, letter to John L. Swain, 5 May 1946.

29 It was written to Smeaton in St Boniface, Manitoba, and the Jesuit catalogues show that Henry was there only for the year 1926–27.

30 Apparently he read the *De anima* in Greek, without discovering there what some years later, maybe under the influence of Thomas Aquinas, he found so engrossing. In fact, he was at first rather critical of Aristotle (see note 49 below).

31 Lonergan still remembered in 1981 his early interest in cognitional theory (*Caring*, pp. 45, 48). Further, his letters to Henry Smeaton in the first flush of studies at Heythrop express enthusiasm for what he was learning. I earlier suggested that his involvement in university courses derailed his initial interest in philosophy. His enthusiasm for Plato seems to have developed later (see note 47 below).

Generally in the prepared paper, '*Insight* revisited', Lonergan speaks more mildly of Heythrop than in the free-wheeling interviews of *Caring*: 'The professors were competent and extremely honest . . . [*Caring* agrees on this, p. 129] I was quite interested in philosophy, but also extremely critical of the key position accorded universal concepts' ('*Insight* revisited', p. 263). Philip Whiteside, who taught most of the first-year philosophy (a professor assigned to teach metaphysics never arrived), made a good impression. 'When he was on Kant, he said, "Now I don't want you to think you have a refutation of Kant; these are just a few pin pricks . . ." But whatever he said was absolutely true' (*Caring*, p. 129). Whiteside sold the idea that there was a problem of knowledge (p. 15), but did not, Lonergan felt, have any solutions (p. 47).

In the absence of a professor of metaphysics, a professor of fundamental theology (perhaps Leonard Geddes) filled in—in a manner. Lonergan was very grateful to him because he gave only three lectures on metaphysics in the whole year, 'So I never had to unlearn all that nonsense' (p. 43).

32 '*Insight* revisited', p. 263.

33 'The form of mathematical inference', *Blandyke Papers* no. 283 (January 1928), pp. 126–37. These *Papers*, being extra-curricular and in a sense 'holiday' work, are named from a village near Liège where the students had their weekly holiday in the years when English laws forced the Jesuit seminary across the English Channel. They were not published but hand-written in a notebook (after being duly refereed) which was left in the College reading-room.

34 'The form of inference', *Thought* 18 (1943), pp. 277–92; republished in *Collection*, pp. 3–16. There is a memory failure in *Caring*, p. 13, where the precursor of this article is said to be a paper with the same title read before the 'Phil and Lit Society'; the title of the paper and

subsequent article in *Blandyke Papers* was 'The syllogism'—it was the precursor of 'The form of inference'.

35   *Caring*, p. 2.

36   'The syllogism', *Blandyke Papers* no. 285 (March 1928), pp. 33-64. There is some evidence that the version in *Thought* was a third draft, that there was a second offered somewhere earlier (and unsuccessfully) for publication; see *Collection*, pp. 256-7.

37   *Caring*, p. 15—a slip of the tongue in the interview locates this experience in Montreal rather than at Heythrop.

38   B. Lonergan, 'The form of inference' in *Collection*, pp. 15-16.

39   'True judgment and science', *Blandyke Papers* no. 291 (February 1929), pp. 195-216. This paper too was an address to the Philosophical and Literary Society; it appears without signature in the *Papers*.

40   Here, at this early stage and in simple form, is the fundamental thrust of Lonergan's lifelong inquiry: what is the human mind? We just saw that his rewrite of 'The syllogism' had 'to do with the nature of the human mind'. His doctoral dissertation will be guided by the simple maxim, 'the human mind is always the human mind' ('The *Gratia Operans* dissertation: preface and introduction', *Method: Journal of Lonergan Studies* 3/2 (October 1985), p. 12), and his whole methodological structure will be erected on the same principle (see Chapter 5 below).

41   I have this information from conversations held with his contemporaries in February 1985, when I was preparing an obituary: Harold Bedford, Fred Elliott (who had it from Bernard's brother, Greg, that Bernard was considering leaving the Order), and Edward Sheridan (who reported that Lonergan told him the question for the regents at Loyola then was not 'Shall we leave the Order?' but 'When shall we leave?').

42   B. Lonergan, letter of January 1935 to Henry Keane, p. 3.

43   *Caring*, p. 32.

44   My source on his teaching mechanics is Edward Sheridan, who was a student at Loyola then (conversation of note 41 above).

45   B. Lonergan, letter to John L. Swain, 24 May 1946.

46   As letters in the Archives attest, many of them maintained a lifelong attachment to their brilliant teacher; several achieved considerable fame in their own right.

47   '*Insight* revisited', pp. 264-5. *Caring* is definite that he read Stewart on Plato when he was at Loyola in the 1930s (pp. 1, 22). See also his 1935 letter to Henry Keane (only two years after regency): 'I got interested in Plato during regency and came to understand him' (p. 3); his understanding was deepened years later through reading Voegelin: 'I had always been given the impression that Plato's dialogues were concerned with pure intellect until I read Dr. Voegelin and learned that they were concerned with social decline, the break-up of the Greek city-states. It was human reasonableness trying to deal with an objective social, political mess' (in E. Cahn and C. Going (eds), *The Question as Commitment: A Symposium* (Montreal, 1977), p. 119); 'I have picked up things [on Plato] from Voegelin that I didn't know before' (*Caring*, p. 48; see also pp. 49, 253, 262). On

Plato as 'the perfect introduction to philosophy', see *Caring*, p. 253.

His interest in Augustine began, it seems, immediately after regency: 'then when I went to the Immaculate to study theology I started reading Augustine there—the dialogues of Cassiciacum' (*Caring*, p. 22); the 1935 letter, much nearer in time to the actual event, locates it in 'the summer before theology' (see n. 49)—presumably late summer, when he was in the theologate but before classes had started.

48 'Gilbert Keith Chesterton', *Loyola College Review* 17 (1931), pp. 7–10; 'The college chapel' (unsigned editorial), ibid., 19 (1933), pp. 1–3. (The previous volume of the *Review* also had an unsigned article on the college chapel; this was erroneously attributed to Lonergan in the first bibliography of his writings, F. E. Crowe (ed.), *Spirit as Inquiry: Studies in Honor of Bernard Lonergan* (Chicago, 1964), p. 244.)

49 B. Lonergan, letter to Henry Keane, 1935, p. 3. The essay does not survive as such in his papers, but it is highly likely that some fragments do: there are thirteen scrap pages (Lonergan had used them as wrappers for other sheaves) of what seems to be a 36-page essay on something like the act of assent; the pages are legal-size, single-space typing, and the length would be about 25,000 words; the fragments clearly belong to his pre-doctorate days: for example, there is a certain scorn for Aristotle, as there was in 'The form of mathematical inference', p. 128, and 'The syllogism', p. 34, while Plato is the favourite; it seems a good guess that they are fragments of the essay mentioned in the 1935 letter.

50 Some circumstances of the decision are related in the quotation I give in the text. More can be added from the oral tradition (John L. Swain): there were two Jesuits from English Canada already in Rome to start theology; they learned that three places in the college were unexpectedly vacant, and since Fr Hingston had asked for five they informed him of the fact; Hingston then decided in mid-semester to transfer three more of his men there. On such flimsy accidents of history are great careers dependent—one thinks of Lonergan's repeated references to luck as a factor in one's life, a luck of course to be related to the *fatum* he found in Thomas Aquinas, and to his fascinating accounts of the Thomist idea of the universal instrumentality of creation under God.

Incidentally, three Jesuit catalogues are in great confusion on Lonergan's status for 1933–34. The Jesuits of French Canada have him in Montreal. Those of English Canada have him in Rome; this is not due to greater efficiency on their part—on the contrary, they were so slow getting their catalogue out that they were able to incorporate the change. The Roman catalogue has Gregory Lonergan instead of Bernard in the house list, p. 24, and the index, p. 95 (with Gregory's dates here); the list of those in Rome from Canada, p. 68, shows neither one nor the other, but the Scholastic Bernardus Nonergan in first-year theology. But Jesuit catalogues were published in the fall, early or late, depending on the office staff, and Lonergan's change from Montreal to Rome took place in November. He told me once (conversation of 17 February 1975) that he had arrived in Rome three weeks late for classes (the University *Kalendarium* has classes starting that year on 3 November), and a Christmas card to Henry Smeaton shows Lonergan still new to the city of Rome.

51　But here, as elsewhere, the pattern is not simple: it is the same relationship, akin to love-hate, that we have found in earlier periods of his life. We shall see the evidence for this in the text, but it may be noted now that the relationship with Rome and the Gregorian University was aggravated by his return to teach there years later. 'I taught theology for twenty-five years under impossible conditions': *Philosophy of God, and Theology: The Relationship between Philosophy of God and the Functional Specialty, Systematics* (St Michael's Lectures, Gonzaga University, Spokane, 1972; London/Philadelphia, 1973), p. 15. Twelve of these years were in Rome, where 'the situation I was in was hopelessly antiquated, but had not yet been demolished—it has since been demolished': 'An Interview with Fr. Bernard Lonergan, S.J.' in *A Second Collection*, p. 212.

52　This little library of classics was still in Lonergan's possession when he was teaching theology in Montreal: the late John Hochban, who was a student there from 1940 to 1944 and himself a classicist, told me of borrowing some volumes and finding them copiously marked and annotated. It is a pity that the collection has been lost, perhaps in the packing of his books and papers at the Gregorian University in 1965–66, for he was not able to supervise this.

53　There are three pieces in this correspondence: a postcard sent on arrival (Lonergan had forgotten his alarm clock—would Henry send it?), a Christmas card which must have followed soon after, and the long letter of 9 May 1934. (I have corrected minor faults of grammar in quoting these and other letters.)

　　We are fortunate that his impressions of Rome survived half a century. We are not so well informed on his impressions of Europe, though we know he visited Florence (*Caring*, p. 222), Bruges and Ghent, the Louvre and the London National Gallery (ibid., p. 223). He lectured once on the national mentalities of Europe (in Montreal, 1941), but only his sketchy notes and a news report remain on that (Archives). His summer assignment on completing theology in 1937 was to the Jesuit parish in Accrington, England (*Caring*, p. 157), and his 1938 letter to Henry Keane was written from Milltown Park, Dublin, where he was preparing to give his first retreat (to the Loretto Sisters in Wexford). A short wartime article, 'The Queen's Canadian Fund' (*The Montreal Beacon*, 11 April 1941, p. 2), begins: 'I was preaching a retreat to a community of nuns in the south-coast town of Worthing, some miles west of Brighton, when the theory of the Blitzkrieg was first put to the test on the Poles'.

54　B. Lonergan, letter to Henry Keane, 22 January 1935; see note 9 above.

55　B. Lonergan, another letter to Henry Keane, still his provincial superior, dated 10 August 1938; see note 53 above.

56　The file is numbered 713 in Lonergan's rather careful arrangement of

35

his papers, but it was not found in place in the cabinet of numbered folders when I packed his papers in November 1983; it may have been somewhere in the confusion of materials lying here and there in his Boston College room. The late John Hochban made a preliminary catalogue of these when we brought them to Toronto, and came upon this precious file. It bears the one-word title 'History'.

Lonergan's notes on Toynbee can be readily dated as made somewhat later. First, the paper used is the size much favoured at L'Immaculée-Conception, where Lonergan taught from 1940 to 1946. More decisive is the witness of *Caring*, p. 88: 'When I was teaching at L'Immaculée Conception I read the first six volumes of Toynbee's *A Study of History* in the long winter evenings. (Jim Shaw used to procure them from the McGill library for me.)' Shaw was a student at the College from 1940 to 1942, the likely period for his performing this library service.

Four other (single) pages of bibliography in the file are on Gerald Heard, Nicolas Berdyaev, Emile Brehier, and J. Huizinga (the latter two from a *Festschrift* for Ernst Cassirer).

57   I follow the description of the Hochban catalogue. There are 31 pages clipped together. The first two have the title 'Sketch for a metaphysic of human solidarity'. On the third page is a quotation from Thomas Aquinas, Ia, 85, 3 c., followed by a table of contents under the title *Pantôn Anakephalaiôsis*. Then follows a 3-page preface, and the next 25 pages are titled '*Pantôn Anakephalaiôsis*—A theory of human solidarity'. To be grouped with these pieces is a sheaf of five unnumbered pages with the same title, *Pantôn Anakephalaiôsis*, to which is added by hand, 'in terms of about 20 ideas, not proved!'—evidently meant as a synopsis, made before or after writing the main essay. My references will be to the main, dated item.

There are two pages of remarks by a critic. Who was he? The phrase 'by Jove' on his second page suggests an Englishman, and a reasonable guess is Fr Bernard Leeming; Lonergan did considerable work on the footnotes of Leeming's Christology book (oral communication from John L. Swain, who was a fellow-student of Lonergan's in Rome), was a good friend and refers to him with respect in '*Insight* revisited' (pp. 265, 276). But L. Keeler, also a good friend, had been reading some of Lonergan's essays (from a conversation I had with the latter, 16 March 1964); would Keeler, an American, write 'by Jove' in his critique? A third but distant possibility is Fr Eric Smith who revised the Latin of Lonergan's review of Keeler.

58   B. Lonergan, '*Insight* revisited', pp. 271–2.

59   I am helped here by the suggestions of Michael Shute; on the basis of internal evidence he divides the papers into two batches, an earlier group that include *Pantôn Anakephalaiôsis*, and a later that deal directly with history; see his doctoral dissertation, 'The origins of Lonergan's notion of the dialectic of history: a study of Lonergan's early writings on history, 1933–1938', Regis College, 1991.

60   Sixteen typewritten pages numbered 2–17. The pages were clipped together with a note attached reading 'ANALYTIC CONCEPT OF HISTORY. (Return to Father Lonergan)'—as described in the

Hochban catalogue. Michael Shute regards it as the latest paper in the set—not counting, of course, the bibliographic notes on Toynbee *et al*. The attached note supports this view—Lonergan was lending it to someone, and would presumably use his final draft for the purpose.

61 Thirty-six loose typewritten pages numbered 95–130; Michael Shute would date it with the earlier papers in the set.

62 What was that longer work? What did pages 1–94 contain? Did other 'chapters' follow page 130? As John Hochban found the papers, there was a single page with the hand-written title 'Essay in fundamental sociology', and a long quotation in Greek from Plato's *Republic*, followed immediately by the pages (95–130) of 'Philosophy of history'; the latter could have been a chapter, then, in the 'Essay'.

63 Lonergan's reference to 'our discussion of economics' is intriguing. Is he referring to something in the pages we have, or in the lost pages that may have followed page 130? And how much work had he done on economics at this time? The 1935 letter to Henry Keane says he has completed a draft of 'a Thomistic metaphysic of history' that deals, among other things, with 'the "objective and inevitable laws" of economics, of psychology . . . and of progress' (p. 5). Is this the *Pantôn* paper given to his critic three months later? Is there a paper, or was there a paper, dealing more specifically with economics? In any case his interest in economics went back to his Heythrop days and his return to a Canada deep in the world economic depression (*Caring*, pp. 30–1). In *Question as Commitment* (see note 47 above) he says: 'From 1930 to about 1944 I spent a great deal of my free time on economic theory' (p. 110).

64 To Hitler, the Spanish Civil War, England's role as the balance of power for the Continent; to the social teaching of the Church, liberalism and Bolshevism; to Dawson, where Lonergan is forced to rely on memory; to 'the chaos of international diplomacy'; and, for an example of Catholic questions of current interest, to the importance of auricular confession to keep sin labelled as sin. This sampling reinforces the need to see Lonergan's intellectualist period in terms of withdrawal and return, where the withdrawal is only strategic.

65 I borrow this application of the term 'apprentice' from William Mathews.

66 From the 1938 Catalogue of the Champagne Province of French Jesuits. They are still having trouble with his Irish name: three times it appears in the Catalogue as 'Longeran'—they are at least consistent.

67 The reference we saw to the years 1937–38 for the start of his interest in history raises the question whether he wrote some of the papers of File 713 during tertianship. It is possible that he did, but tertianship was not regarded as a year for that kind of exercise; and there are the summers of 1937 and 1938 when he might well have done some of the papers, though he was occupied in both periods with priestly ministry (note 53 above).

He told me (conversation of 30 August 1964) that after one year of his biennium, hence in 1939, he had asked permission of Father General, on the ground of his mother's illness, to go home for the summer, and had been refused. It may be that he had asked already in the summer of 1938; see the letter of 10 August 1938, to Fr Henry Keane: 'It was very kind of you to write Greg about my not coming home; and while we are on the personal theme, I had a splendid letter from my mother the other day, and that pulls a cloud out of the sky'. But the cloud returned and was dark indeed; nearly 40 years later he could write: 'The death of your mother keeps reminding me of the death of mine. It was in February 1940. I had been in Europe since November 1933. Fr Vincent McCormick Rector of the Gregorian broke the news to me. He did it very nicely, but I did not speak for three days. I guess I was in a minor state of shock' (letter of 21 December 1976, to F. E. Crowe).

His letters home during his seven-year absence, which his mother kept till her death (unfortunately, they were then destroyed), would have been a mine of information on his activities in this period, but we do not know whether he even mentioned the essays he was drafting then.

68 In '*Insight* revisited', p. 266, he records advice he received on reconciling obedience and initiative in his religious Order: 'Go ahead and do it. If superiors do not stop you, that is obedience. If they do stop you, stop and that is obedience.'

69 There is something of Lonergan's characteristic fatalism in this whole matter, as there was throughout the years he taught theology. He was not a rebel in the usual sense, demanding new curricula before he knew what was needed; so he continued to teach theology for 25 years 'under impossible conditions', more concerned with the long-range future than with present courses.

70 The history of these negotiations provides another sample of luck, fate, providence in the life of Bernard Lonergan. The Jesuit General had exhorted his 'assembled provincials to donate men to the Gregorian University. The Upper Canadian provincial . . . donated me. I was informed of this at the end of tertianship and told to do a biennium in philosophy. The following September, however, I had a letter from Fr Vincent McCormick informing me that most of the English-speaking students at the Gregorian were in theology and that I, accordingly, was to do a biennium in theology' ('*Insight* revisited', p. 266). A piece of the history is a letter from Fr McCormick to Henry Keane, dated 20 July 1938 (Archives of the Lonergan Research Institute):

> Fr Lonergan has left a splendid record behind him here; and we shall be happy to see him back for further studies. I would suggest —supposing his own preferences are not too strong for one field rather than the other—that he devote himself to Theology. In that Faculty there are hundreds of English-speaking students, who will be needing his help in the future.

There is no evidence that Lonergan's 'preferences' were consulted. Probably he was happy with the substance of the decision, though his reminiscences suggest a certain dislike of the way it was reached.

2

Apprentice to Thomas Aquinas: 'eleven years of my life'

FIRST CASUAL ENCOUNTER

A current view on Lonergan's development assumes that he began as a disciple of Thomas Aquinas and went on in *Insight* to integrate modern thought with that of Thomas. I contributed to this myth when I wrote once: 'An account of the sources of *Insight* reduces . . . to two . . . headings: the Thomism at its basis, and those features of the last seven centuries of thought which have been integrated into Thomism'.[1]

That was in 1957. Some of us might have corrected our mistake next year, when we heard Lonergan say in the Halifax lectures: 'My philosophic development was from Newman to Augustine, from Augustine to Plato, and then I was introduced to Thomism through . . . Stephanou'.[2] Ten years later we all had a corrective when Lonergan was asked in regard to *Insight* 'whether my prior allegiance to Thomism did not predetermine the results I reached' in that book; his reply was deceptively mild: 'Now it is true that I spent a great deal of time in the study of St Thomas and that I know I owe a great deal to him. I just add, however, that my interest in Aquinas came late.'[3]

Newman has taught us that apprehension can be real or it can be merely notional, and I suspect it was the latter way in which we apprehended Lonergan's statements on his own intellectual history. It was only recently, on the basis of documents from his early life, those we examined in Chapter 1, that we could see how deeply involved he was with sociology and history, with Hegel and Marx

39

rather than with Aristotle and Thomas, and only then could we come to a real apprehension of his encounter with Thomas Aquinas. With that real apprehension we are able to see the very significant shift in tactics, maybe even the very radical shift in strategy, that *Insight* shows over the studies in the *Blandyke Papers* and in File 713. Had he written his masterpiece on leaving Heythrop, he might have been seen as an imitator of Hume, ready to take on the philosophic universe at the age of 26; had he written it on leaving Amiens, it might have been to challenge Hegel with another view of world history. In any case it would not have been *Insight* that emerged; to write that work, he needed a real encounter with Thomas Aquinas; instead of starting his career as a new luminary, he needed instead to become a disciple, a learner, an apprentice.

The first step in the encounter has been described: in Montreal in the summer and fall of 1933 he did some first-hand reading and 'began to suspect that St Thomas was not nearly as bad as he is painted'. The suspicion was verified in his studies under Bernard Leeming two or three years later: 'I first discovered that Saint Thomas might have something to say when I was taught "De Verbo Incarnato" in Rome'.[4] Leeming and Stephanou seem to have disposed him favourably toward Thomas, but he had not yet begun the apprenticeship of which he says in *Insight* that it 'changed me profoundly', an apprenticeship in which he spent 'years reaching up to the mind of Aquinas'.[5] Later he will define this period more closely: 'about eleven years of my life'.[6] So up to 1938 his interest was not enough to turn him from his sociology and history; his Montreal reading of Thomas and the Roman influence of Leeming and Stephanou left him well disposed to Thomas, but their full effect was felt only a few years later.

FROM READER TO DISCIPLE

I have recounted the accident of history that sent him to the Gregorian University for doctoral studies in theology, when for the five preceding years he had read and thought and wrote in the expectation of studying philosophy. So he set out for Rome in the fall of 1938 apparently without a definite idea on an area and a theme for his doctoral dissertation.

Did he think of pursuing the ideas he had worked on in File 713? It would be surprising if he did not, but we have documentation only for the choice of Charles Boyer as director for his thesis and for the way they hit upon a theme in St Thomas. He had asked advice in France on a director, and been told that Boyer was an intelligent person, proved by the fact that he could change his mind—he had done so on the real distinction between essence and existence![7] Boyer agreed to direct him, and they discussed different topics only to set them aside. Finally Boyer reached out for his *Summa* Ia IIae, opened it at an article on *gratia operans*, and said: 'Here is an article that I don't know how to interpret, one on which I've consulted authors and commentaries in vain, one that doesn't seem to lend itself to either a Molinist or a Banezian reading. Take this article, if you like. Study the *loca parallela* and the historical sources. See what light you can shed on the question.'[8] Classes that year began in earnest only on 7 November, and a month later on 6 December Lonergan's thesis topic is listed in the university records as approved under the title 'A history of St Thomas's thought on operative grace'.[9]

Lonergan may have needed the eleven years for reaching up to the mind of Thomas, but a much shorter time converted him from a student favourably disposed into a lifelong disciple. Publishing his study of Thomas on grace he could not conceal his enthusiasm: 'the new wine of speculative theology is bursting the old bottles of Pelagian controversy'.[10] His concluding summary speaks of Thomist thought on grace as but

> an incident in the execution of a far vaster program. If on the surface that program was to employ the Aristotelian scientific technique against the die-hard traditionalism of the current Christian Platonists and, at the same time, to inaugurate historical research by appealing to the real Aristotle against the Parisian Averroists, in point of fact no less than in essence it was to lay under tribute Greek and Arab, Jew and Christian, in an ever renewed effort to obtain for Catholic culture that *aliquam intelligentiam eamque fructuosissimam* which is the goal of theological speculation.[11]

The mood persists into 1949 and the concluding pages of the *verbum* study, where he says of Thomas and his intellectualism that he did not get lost 'in the Platonist fog'—Aristotle has replaced Plato, at least in cognitional theory—but 'steadily progressed from the *Sentences* towards the clear and calm, the economic and functional, the balanced and exact series of questions and articles of the *via doctrinae* in the *Summa*, in which the intellectualism of

Aristotle, made over into the intellectualism of St Thomas, shines as unmistakably as the sun on the noonday summer hills of Italy'.[12] Nor does he think the role of Thomas ceased with the Middle Ages: 'A completely genuine development of the thought of St Thomas will command in all the universities of the modern world the same admiration and respect that St Thomas himself commanded in the medieval University of Paris'.[13]

This belief is repeated in his own masterwork, *Insight*, where, after declaring his years of 'reaching up to the mind of Aquinas' and the way 'that reaching had changed me profoundly', he goes on to speak of Thomas and the modern world in terms that are still fully positive, if somewhat less lyrical than before: 'it is only through a personal appropriation of one's own rational self-consciousness that one can hope to reach the mind of Aquinas and, once that mind is reached, then it is difficult not to import his compelling genius to the problems of this later day'.[14] But what we should import, and how we should retail it now, are questions we will consider later in this chapter.

DOCTORAL DISSERTATION: APPRENTICE IN THE THEOLOGY OF GRACE

It would be a mistake to see Lonergan's work on grace in terms of the sixteenth-century controversy between the Dominican Domingo Báñez and the Jesuit Luis de Molina. True, he had to shed his Molinist views as completely as his Jesuit training had taught him to dispose of Báñez: 'I had been brought up a Molinist. I was studying St Thomas's Thought on *Gratia Operans* . . . Within a month or so it was completely evident to me that Molinism had no contribution to make to an understanding of Aquinas.'[15] But later controversies were not the question, and he defined his approach to Thomas in terms that would be acceptable to the most rigorous positivist:

We are not engaged in proposing a theory in speculative theology. We are giving an account of someone else's theories. And in that task we are not concerned with the implications of his position, the ulterior development of his position, or even the defence of his position. We ask what he said, why he said it and what he meant in saying it.[16]

Setting out to give some account of this dissertation I cannot myself avoid a very personal approach. I carry the freight of my own apprenticeship to Lonergan, four years when I sat as a disciple at the feet of a master, and this just at the time when he was fresh from his study of grace in Thomas and engrossed in his work on Thomist cognitional theory. That experience I have to regard as an incalculable asset in understanding both Lonergan and Thomas, but I have to recognize also that I can too easily identify my personal growth with the gains I see Lonergan bringing to the wider theological universe.

With that caution, I present the following points as samples only of what Lonergan's study of grace in Thomas meant to me and may contribute to a wider theology. There is the Thomist psychology which I found so deeply explanatory of and clearly verifiable in my religious experience that I could not regard it as of merely archaeological interest. There is the notion that joins divine transcendence and human activity, the elusive and fascinating idea of universal instrumentality, the link between the Hebrew sense of God at work in all events, and the Greek philosophy of forms and forces at work in nature. Add the account of habitual grace in Thomas and its need for correcting our moral impotence: man's 'higher powers are the spiritual counterpart of *materia prima*, and their indeterminate potentiality points at once in all directions', but 'give man the virtues and in place of the statistical law governing humanity one will have an approximation to the statistical law governing the angels'.[17] Add too the divine operation that goes beyond the virtues to take control of our lives: 'just as wisdom for us is not understanding but faith, so the highest perfection of man cannot be immanent as are the virtues, but rather must link us dynamically with the sole source of absolute perfection'.[18]

I feel bound to say also that this experience, of studying divine grace under Lonergan, was an experience of hearing a doctrine that had taken possession of its teacher. There was conviction in Lonergan's voice, even when he adduced proof-texts in the ahistorical manner of older theology, even when the Scripture he read in proof was from the Latin Vulgate. Those texts rang with feeling. If in some of them human freedom was fully recognized (how not, in Molina's Jesuit Order?), it was divine efficacy that came through as bedrock: *Cor regis in manu Domini* (Prov 21: 1); *non volentis, neque currentis, sed miserentis est Dei* (Rom 9: 16); *cum metu et tremore vestram salutem operamini. Deus est enim, qui operatur in vobis et velle et perficere pro bona voluntate* (Phil 2: 12–13). For a striking index of the depth of Lonergan's conviction on this point I refer again to the way he ended chapter 20 of *Insight*: speaking of the search for the truth, he tells his readers not to feel they are alone, for what they seek 'is principally the work of God who illuminates our intellects . . . who breaks the bonds of our habitual unwillingness . . . by inspiring the hope . . . by infusing the charity, the love, that bestows on intelligence the fullness of life'.[19]

What I am saying about the grace dissertation, and would repeat for the *verbum* articles, is that it is the experiential side that brings the metaphysics to life. For both studies are full of metaphysics: act and potency, essence and existence, matter and form, *actio* and *passio*, substance and accidents, being, causes, immateriality, things. This is not merely incidental to his teaching. It was metaphysics that gave solidity to his teeming thought in both areas, and his grasp of Thomist metaphysics went hand in hand with his discovery of Thomist psychology. Though he will later make metaphysics derivative, that is, give it a critical foundation in cognitional theory, he will not discard it: it retains its function 30 years later in his *Method in Theology*.[20]

I have indulged in some quite personal recollections. Let me, before closing this brief account of Lonergan's work on grace, turn more objectively to ideas that bear directly on controversies today.

One is Lonergan's view of divine transcendence, 'that God knows with equal infallibility, He wills with equal irresistibility, He effects with equal efficacy, both the necessary and the contingent'.[21] The last six words contain the key. It is easy enough to affirm in a general way divine omniscience and divine omnipotence, but we must relate them to the human world. Now necessity and contingence denote relations *within* the created world: the sun necessarily melts the ice, I contingently chose the example of sun and ice as I wrote. These relations are in contradictory opposition to one another: 'contingent' ('free' in this context) contradicts 'necessary' or 'not free', and vice versa. But both sun and I, besides the opposed relations we have to our effects, derive our power and our activity from God in a way that is *outside* that pair of contradictories; God has a role in the two activities, the sun's melting and my choosing, that transcends both necessity and contingence. The root of difficulties about divine efficacy is the attempt to bring it within the categories that apply to created agencies, where it must be either necessary or contingent; in fact, it lies outside those categories. I call this Lonergan's view, but it is right out of Thomas's commentary on Aristotle's *Peri Hermeneias*, the best locus on the question that I have found in him, and certainly a favourite of Lonergan.

His definition of divine transcendence does not mention time and foreknowledge—a problem that has emerged again in our own day, and exercises philosophers so much—for the very good reason that the problem is not urgent there. The Thomist commentary on Aristotle treats it as a separate question and disposes of it on the simple basis that nothing is future to God; in short, there is no *fore*knowledge of contingent events, either human or divine. But that does not touch the real difficulty; even if time is disposed of, the real difficulty remains. Entirely apart from the question of foreknowledge, here and now in this present moment, how can my action be free if God's action is efficacious? That question is independent of questions of time, and reveals the point of application of the doctrine of divine transcendence: necessity and contingence, as we understand them, simply are not transferrable to God, whose relation to divine effects lies outside that pair. That is the crucial point, though of course we must also dispose of the element of priority in time and affirm a simultaneity that is special to the divine operation: 'It is only in the logico-metaphysical simultaneity of the atemporal present that God's knowledge is infallible, His will irresistible, His action efficacious'.[22]

A second idea in a currently controversial area is the theorem of the supernatural. It was not especially a Thomist discovery, but Lonergan credits Thomas with exploiting it through the range of theology: 'in the writings of St. Albert or St. Thomas, the *supernatural* is a scientific theorem'.[23] This question has wide ramifications. What is needed here, and cannot be provided in the space I have, is to follow Lonergan's history of the way the natural-supernatural distinction arose, to set forth his understanding of the distinction, to study its ramifications in theology. My compromise solution is to give my own synoptic view of the relationship and its history, offering it as an interpretation, but not undertaking the dissertation of doctoral dimensions needed to establish it as valid either in itself or as a view of what Lonergan held.

One begins with God and the problem consequent on God's decision to share the divine being with others. Any such other being will, of course, be conceived from the beginning as a unit, and the unity of conception will govern the unity of realization. But it is precisely that unity that is God's problem. On the one hand there will be a sharing in the infinite being of God, and on the other there is as yet nothing outside of God, something must be created, and so there will necessarily be a finite creation that shares in the infinite: a composite and disproportionately constituted creation is involved in the very idea of a creation that shares the divine being. It cannot be a unity with the unity of God. There will be a line drawn, a distinction between what something is of itself and what that something is in its sharing of the infinite.

This does not decide whether in fact a completely 'natural' being ever exists: it may be true that all the things that are, are created in the state in which they already share the divine. But that does not eliminate the two components, the sharing and the shared, of the things that are; neither does it eliminate the laws that are 'natural' to the sharing component: we do not expect grapes from thorns nor figs from thistles. This is true even if a being is created open to the infinite in a way thorns and thistles are not: it will be a nature in an analogous sense, it will be *such* as to be open to the infinite. Something like that, I believe, is the way Lonergan saw the supernatural order.

The history of our discovery of this order can be set forth with a like brevity. First, for the early Church there was just the undifferentiated whole: one God, one world, one compact order. Difficulties with the undifferentiated view led to the distinction drawn in 1225 by Philip the Chancellor who 'presented the theory of two orders, entitatively disproportionate: not only was there the familiar series of grace, faith, charity and merit, but also nature, reason and the natural love of God'.[24] Distinction led inevitably to separation, and so with the passing centuries to the idea of an independent natural order. This order was conceived not only as possible and self-contained but as an existing unit in reality, to which existing unit the supernatural was then added—and so we get all the drawbacks, the anomalies, the poverty, of an extrinsicist theology, that is, of a theology in which divine grace is extrinsic to the human way of being.

Still, absurdity evokes a healthy reaction. As distinction had led unhappily to separation, so separation led more happily to efforts to see the inner relationship, in this one world that exists, of the components that are a unit in the original divine idea. We are able now in the twentieth century to see our world as one, as of course our ancestors did, but with an understanding they could not achieve without going through the same steps of distinction, separation, relationship in union, that history has provided for us.

Such, as I conceive it, is the way Lonergan's views on the supernatural order and on the history of its discovery can be set forth. One has to grasp

that the idea of the supernatural is a theorem, that it no more adds to the data of the problem than the Lorentz transformation

puts a new constellation in the heavens. What Philip the Chan-
ellor systematically posited was . . . the validity of a line of
reference termed nature. In the long term and in the concrete
the real alternatives remain charity and cupidity . . . But the
whole problem lies in the abstract, in human thinking: the fallacy
in early thought had been an unconscious confusion of the metaphysical abstraction, nature, with concrete data which do not
quite correspond; Philip's achievement was the creation of a
mental perspective, the introduction of a set of coordinates,
that eliminated the basic fallacy and its attendant host of
anomalies.[25]

What did Lonergan learn from this study of Thomas? It was,
after all, a doctoral dissertation, and a dissertation is a learning
exercise as well as (one hopes) a contribution to the academy. Too
many doctoral candidates, I believe, ignore that more humble role
of a dissertation; they aim at a world-shaking production, only to
find in the end that the world remains unshaken, and that they have
squandered the best years of their lives on a rather fruitless idea.
Lonergan's own formula for a dissertation was 'What X says about
Y'—to which I would add, 'Let X be a thinker of stature and Y be a
manageably small question'. The thinker of stature will stretch the
candidate's mind, and a question that is manageable may not shake
the world but can very well introduce candidates to the corpus, say,
of Aquinas and to the way Aquinas worked, and as well open up a
personal career of lasting import.

I would apply this to Lonergan. His doctoral work may have been
quite exceptional. Nevertheless, the gain, I believe, was not there;
the real value of his dissertation lay less in points of objective theology than in factors that are more subjective and methodological,
factors that for this very reason are far more fundamental; in this
respect the influence of Lonergan's doctoral work on his subsequent
development can hardly be exaggerated. His real discovery was of
the way Aquinas worked and questioned and thought and understood and thought again and judged and wrote. One cannot document such a gain by pointing to a particular work or idea, and in any
case the gain is rarely definitive: always one is 'reaching up to the
mind of Aquinas'.

If that is the case, we can hardly expect that interpreters will agree
on what the master means:

. . . the greater such a genius is, perhaps the more varied will be
the schools that appeal to him; for it is not to be taken for granted

that the ever lesser followers of genius will be capable of ascending more than halfway up the mountain of his achievement or even, at times, of recognizing that one mountain has many sides.[26]

Now that quotation serves a double purpose. It not only clarifies the situation among Thomists, it is also a fine symbol of, and analogy for, what Thomas and all of us are doing: reaching up to the mind of God.

With that we come to the greatest single benefit Lonergan derived from his encounter with Thomas: his sense of God as mystery. Here in the transcendence of divine operation on free human wills, a little later in the mystery of the trinitarian processions, and through his life to *Method in Theology* and beyond, in the welter of words that with other theologians it was his vocation to utter, Lonergan never lost what Thomas above all theologians could teach, that theology can be done, must be done, that when it is done, we are confronted with mystery and bow our heads in adoration.[27]

APPRENTICESHIP PROLONGED: THOMIST COGNITIONAL THEORY

The transformation has been great indeed, from one who browsed rather indifferently in Aquinas, suspecting he was not as bad as he was painted, to the one who wrote the lines I have been quoting from his dissertation. The experience must have been overpowering, for it deflected him from his early ambition for several more years while he continued his apprenticeship. Various new areas of study are worth noticing—for example, the concept of order in Thomas[28]—but interpreters tend to focus, as I will do, on the area that assumed such importance in the sequel: Thomist cognitional theory.

Cognitional theory had caught Lonergan's interest at Heythrop College, was a factor in the papers of File 713 (where he took a Thomist text on developing knowledge as a kind of motto for his work in sociology[29]), and figured largely in the long-unpublished introduction to his dissertation.[30] So there was a seminal interest in cognitional theory, and indeed a particular interest in the Thomist form, that lay fallow for ten years. He has his own helpful account of the way the seed germinated:

In 1933 I had been much struck by an article of Peter Hoenen's in *Gregorianum* arguing that intellect abstracted from phantasm

48

not only terms but also the nexus between them. He held that that certainly was the view of Cajetan and probably of Aquinas. Later he returned to the topic, arguing first that Scholastic philosophy was in need of a theory of geometrical knowledge, and secondly producing various geometrical illustrations . . . that fitted in very well with his view that not only terms but also nexus were abstracted from phantasm. So about 1943 I began collecting materials for an account of Aquinas' views on understanding and the inner word. The result was a series of articles that appeared in *Theological Studies* from 1946 to 1949.[31]

The articles are known as a study of Thomist cognitional theory, which is indeed what the body of the work is, but the context is trinitarian theology, and specifically the eternal procession of the Holy Spirit. Readers of the book where the articles were published some years later may have been puzzled by the sudden and unexplained appearance of trinitarian questions in the last chapter. The puzzle is solved by three introductory paragraphs, found in the first article but omitted from the book, that had given the context, suggesting that the prevailing obscurity on the procession of the Spirit may be due to obscurity on the eternal procession of the Word; the procession of the Word, however, involves us in cognitional theory; and so that is where the book starts.[32]

This context should not be forgotten. Theologically, the articles are a study of the life of God in its internal dynamism and movement. But philosophically, they are a study of human life in its internal dynamism and movement on the level of spirit, that is, in the twofold procession of inner word and love, and so, to return to theology, in the image of God.

Lonergan uses the word 'rationality' for this interior life of the spirit, but his rationality has nothing to do with the deductive rationalism of some modern philosophers. Quite the contrary; in fact, his chief adversaries are the conceptualists who, if not 'rationalist' in the scholastic world, are strongly deductivist. As Lonergan defined them, they began with concepts, then combined concepts into propositions, and thirdly joined proposition to proposition to construct a syllogism. It might all be quite valid, but there was a great gap, not so much in the system as in its origin, namely, the source of its concepts, and in its existential reference, namely, the ground of its judgements. This Lonergan found in the *intelligere* of Augustine and Thomas, the understanding which in its two levels is the fertile origin and ground of all concepts, judgements and syllogisms. Instead of an 'intellection' which was a metaphysical machine producing concepts without conscious awareness of its ground, he discovered in understanding a power that at every stage of the process was aware of itself, its own dynamism, and its own fertile procedures. It unfolded in two steps: the direct understanding of 'insight into phantasm' producing meaningful concepts, and the reflective understanding of Newman's illative sense grounding concrete judgements. This was 'rationality' for Lonergan.[33]

Under three headings he distinguishes this rational process from natural process. The intelligibility of the latter is passive and potential: 'it is what can be understood; it is not an understanding'. It is 'the intelligibility of some specific natural law . . . but never the intelligibility of the very idea of intelligible law'. And, thirdly, it 'is imposed from without: natures act intelligibly, not because they are intelligent . . . but because they are concretions of divine ideas and a divine plan'. Quite different is the intelligibility of the procession of an inner word: not passive and potential, but

> active and actual . . . intelligible, not as the possible object of understanding is intelligible, but as understanding itself and the activity of understanding is intelligible. Again, its intelligibility defies formulation in any specific law . . . the procession of an inner word is the pure case of intelligible law . . . Thirdly, it is native and natural for the procession of inner word to be intelligible . . . for intelligence in act does not follow laws imposed from without, but rather it is the ground of the intelligibility in act of law, it is constitutive and, as it were, creative of law . . .[34]

Readers of *Insight* may have noticed there the recurring phrase, insight and formulation, without realizing that Lonergan had already given a book-length exposition of its meaning. It is *Verbum* that reveals the rich content of the phrase, that shows us something of the wealth of conscious 'reasoning' activity, of the 'rational process', that enters into the production of a concept, a formulation, a law, a theory.

Of course, this focal point involved the study of the whole complex of cognitional process; it is useful to remember here that 'knowing' was for Lonergan a compound of distinct and different activities. 'Insight into phantasm' became famous as a characteristic feature of his thought; it was the first cognitional activity to be studied in the articles, it gave a name to his most famous work, and the Aristotelian counterpart graces the title-page of that book. But the conceptualization consequent on insight, the reflective inquiry consequent on concepts, and the judgement that issues from reflective understanding—all these elements have to be seen in themselves and in their mutual relation. Then we come to positions on epistemology, objectivity, reality, which also are taken in the *verbum* studies, though they are elaborated much more in *Insight*.

Other topics we find on running through the index of *Verbum*: abstraction, consciousness, criteriology, data, definition, development, emanation, ideas, inquiry and wonder, introspection, learning, light of intellect, logic, love, meaning, mystery, names, objects, operations, phantasm, presence, principles, proportion, questions, quiddity, realism, relations, reflection, science, self-knowledge, soul, subject, synthesis, theology, truth, universal, will, wisdom, wonder, word. Every one of these needs its own monograph, but the mere listing serves a purpose: it may alert us to the complexity of Lonergan's conceptuality (not to be confused with conceptualism), what the Germans would call his *Begrifflichkeit*, at this stage of his development. We shall return to this list in Chapter 6 and see it as a stage on the way to the thought-patterns characteristic of his later work.

I have not included the metaphysical terms that we saw in the dissertation and find again here. They occur now with a difference, for Lonergan has been struggling with the relationship between psychology and metaphysics in the study of Thomas, with the following result:

> I have begun, not from the metaphysical framework, but from the psychological content of Thomist theory of intellect: logic might favor the opposite procedure but, after attempting it in a variety of ways, I found it unmanageable.[35]

He is well on the way to the position so characteristic of *Insight*, in which metaphysics is a corollary of cognitional theory.

IS THE LATER LONERGAN THOMIST?

The title of this section is in the form of a question. There are those who would not only answer it with a flat no but would object strongly to the assumption of an earlier Thomism tacit in the question; they

51

would say that not even the early Lonergan was Thomist, and we shall presently see that he himself did not wish to be 'Thomist' in the manner of classical Thomism. There are those again who find 'transcendental Thomist' a neat pigeon-hole, and file Lonergan away under that heading, though Lonergan himself did not accept that categorization.[36]

The sensible thing, as always with an original thinker, is to study what he did, and then, if labels are needed, apply the ones that fit, or create new ones if the old are unsuitable. I would, in anticipation, state my own view of his general position somewhat as follows. With the passing of the years and his firmer grasp of human historicity, of historical consciousness, of the differentiations of consciousness that distinguish one age in history from another and one group of people from another, Lonergan would see in better perspective the whole of cultural history and Thomas's place in it, but he never lost his enthusiasm for what Thomas had done in his time and from his thirteenth century signals to us as what we must do in the twentieth. But that general position emerged gradually, and it will be useful to look at some of the steps on the way.

Lonergan speaks, at the end of *Insight*, of importing the 'compelling genius' of Aquinas 'to the problems of this later day'. He wrote that remark in 1953, and a year later claims that Thomist 'notions of science seem . . . to be adequate for a formulation of the nature of speculative theology'.[37] Next year he wrote on the 'Isomorphism of Thomist and scientific thought'; he did so with evident respect for Thomas but he concludes, as had been the case a few years earlier in the *verbum* articles, with a plea for work on the *nova* in the phrase he took as a motto from Pope Leo XIII, *vetera novis augere et perficere*: to enlarge and complete the old by addition of the new.[38]

Given his ambitious projects of the 1930s the *nova* could never be really lost to view, but as time went on and he came to a deeper understanding of what they were, his perspective changed. Without losing any of his admiration for Thomas he was able to see that to import the 'compelling genius' of Thomas into our time was not a matter of transferring his ideas word for word across seven centuries; it was more a matter of doing analogously in our time what Thomas did in his.

> . . . besides being a theologian and philosopher St. Thomas was a man of his time meeting the challenge of his time. What he was concerned to do may be viewed as a theological or philosophical synthesis but, if considered more concretely, it

turns out to be a mighty contribution towards the medieval cultural synthesis. As in our day, so too in his there was a feverish intellectual ferment. As in our day we are somewhat belatedly coming to grips with the implications of the modern sciences and philosophies and bringing our theology and Christian living up to date, so too in his day Western Christendom was being flooded with the then novel ideas of Greek and Arabic science and philosophy. As in our day there is a demand for an *aggiornamento* of our thinking, so in his there was a demand for an *aggiornamento* of earlier medieval thought. . . . the magnitude and brilliance of his achievement permit us to single him out as the example . . . of what was going forward in his day, namely, discovering, working out, thinking through a new mould for the Catholic mind, a mould in which it could remain fully Catholic and yet be at home with all the good things that might be drawn from the cultural heritage of Greeks and Arabs.[39]

Lonergan did not, however, have the respect for classical Thomism that he had for Thomas. Under five headings in the same paper he criticizes that school: there was an overemphasis on logic; it took its notion of science from Aristotle's *Posterior Analytics*; it concentrated on the metaphysics of the soul to the neglect of psychological introspection; there was a similar stress on human nature to the neglect of human history; finally, it gave undue weight to first principles. Thomism today must reverse these five trends, not to the exclusion of the interests of classical Thomism, logic, metaphysics, and the rest, but to their subordination to more fundamental factors. The transition, then, will be from logic to method, from an Aristotelian conception of science to a modern, from soul to subject, from human nature to human history, from first principles to transcendental method.[40]

Lonergan, obviously, has kept his youthful dream fresh all these years, and his great purpose of making Catholic thought respectable in a world that by and large scorned it. But there is a personal problem in which his study of Thomas has involved him: on the one hand, his admiration for Thomas was almost boundless; on the other, he could not deny that seven centuries had passed, and that a mere repetition of Thomist ideas would fall now on deaf ears. He had to labour to retain his Thomism and yet live at the level of his time, and as he drew near that level he had to view Thomas from a changing perspective.

Thus in 1955 his paper on isomorphism drew a 'protracted

analogy' between Thomist and scientific thought. He concentrated 'on a structural similarity to prescind entirely from the materials that enter into the structures',[41] and thus to find an isomorphism in nine aspects of scientific and Thomist procedure. But this concern of 1955 reflects Lonergan's effort to bring Catholic thought up to date in the world of natural science, an effort, I shall maintain, more characteristic of his book *Insight* than of his later work on method. It was also an effort that permitted him to retain a closer relationship to Thomas. But it was not sufficient for his later struggle in which he tried to relate the *nova* of the human empirical sciences to the *vetera* of tradition. His 1968 paper on 'The future of Thomism' reflects his concern in that later period, when culture, history, the human sciences were in the foreground, and the analogy regarded not directly the ideas of Thomas but his relation to his culture as 'a man of his time meeting the challenge of his time'.

But analogy was only one way to see our link with Thomas. Lonergan's last public lecture on his master was given in 1974 under the title 'Aquinas today: tradition and innovation'. It is quite definite on the cultural changes that have taken place, but concludes with a few illustrations of the continuity he sees between the Thomist world and ours. It maintains the perspective of an analogy of proportion: what Thomas was to his time we may be to ours, but analogy is only one instance of such continuity. 'First, there is the continuity from the implicit to the explicit', for mediaeval theology was implicitly methodical. 'Secondly, there is continuity in the shift from the Aristotelian ideal of science to the modern reality, for it involves a change more in structure than in content . . . .' 'Thirdly, there is continuity by analogy . . .' in the way both Thomas and our age conceive the world as coming from God, man as the end of the material universe, the meaning and significance of the visible universe as bringing to birth the elect.[42]

Though this paper of 1974 was Lonergan's last major effort to come to terms with Thomas, with Thomism, and with their relevance today, references to Thomas continue to dot the pages of his talks and essays, and even his correspondence. So I return, in conclusion, to the letter of 1980 which gave the present chapter its subtitle. Lonergan referred to the eleven years in which he studied Thomas as years in the functional specialty of research, and went on to say: 'It is from the mind set of research that one most easily learns what Method is about: surmounting differences in history'.[43]

In this brief and almost casual remark we may have the clue for integrating the whole 40 previous years. Lonergan's passion, from first to last, was to join history to systematics (systematics finally understood in the third of the three senses set forth in the 1972 lectures at Spokane, neither Aristotle's system nor that of modern science, but one based on intentionality analysis[44]). Thomas had been an enormous help in developing this third sense of systematics, but the study of Thomas had enabled Lonergan to see him in historical context, and thus to conceive sharply and in all its urgency the problem of overcoming historicity without subordinating it to systematics. That is a problem to take up in later chapters.

Notes

1   F.E. Crowe, 'The origin and scope of Bernard Lonergan's *Insight*' in *Appropriating the Lonergan Idea*, ed. M. Vertin (Washington, DC, 1989), pp. 21–2.

2   B. Lonergan, *Understanding and Being: The Halifax Lectures on Insight*, ed. E.A. Morelli and M.D. Morelli (Toronto, 1990), p. 350. Stephanos Stephanou was a Jesuit of Greek origin, fellow-student of Lonergan's at the Gregorian University; he had previously studied at Louvain, and introduced Lonergan to the work of Maréchal; he afterwards became professor at the Oriental Institute, Rome.

3   B. Lonergan, 'Theories of inquiry: responses to a symposium' in *A Second Collection*, ed. W. Ryan and B. Tyrrell (London/Philadelphia, 1974/1975), p. 38.

4   P. Lambert, C. Tansey and C. Going (eds), *Caring about Meaning: Patterns in the Life of Bernard Lonergan* (Montreal, 1982), p. 258.

5   B. Lonergan, *Insight: A Study of Human Understanding* (London, 1957), p. 748.

6   B. Lonergan, letter to F.E. Crowe, 3 March 1980, referring to his studies of *gratia operans* and the *verbum* in Thomas; the first study began in 1938, the second ended in 1949, giving the 'eleven years'.

7   Information received from Fred Lawrence.

8   B. Lonergan, notes made in preparing to defend his doctoral dissertation, Lonergan Archives, Batch 1-A, Folder 16 (temporary filing).

9   Catalogue I in the Gregorian University file of dissertations.

10   B. Lonergan, *Grace and Freedom: Operative Grace in the Thought of St. Thomas Aquinas*, ed. J.P. Burns (London/New York, 1971), p. 136.

11   Ibid., p. 139.

12   B. Lonergan, *Verbum: Word and Idea in Aquinas*, ed. D. Burrell (Notre Dame, IN/London, 1967/1968), p. 219.

13   Ibid., p. 220.

14   *Insight: A Study of Human Understanding* (2nd edn; London/New York, 1958), p. 748.

15   B. Lonergan, *Method in Theology* (London/New York, 1972), p. 163, n. 5.

16   B. Lonergan, 'The *Gratia Operans* dissertation: preface and

introduction', *Method: Journal of Lonergan Studies* 3/2 (October 1985), p. 15.

17   *Grace and Freedom*, pp. 42, 45.

18   Ibid., p. 44. The preceding paragraph draws on my introduction to the book, pp. ix–xi.

19   *Insight*, p. 730.

20   *Method in Theology*, p. 343 (and see the index to that book, under 'Metaphysics').

21   *Grace and Freedom*, p. 107.

22   Ibid., p. 116. See Thomas Aquinas, *In libros Peri Hermeneias*, Lib. 1, lect. 14.

23   *Grace and Freedom*, p. 13.

24   Ibid., pp. 15–16.

25   Ibid., p. 16.

26   Ibid., p. 140.

27   Divine transcendence is the locus of mystery in the dissertation, but mystery is discussed only briefly in relation to sin and intelligibility (p. 113); still, it is assumed throughout and those who have followed Lonergan's course on divine grace can easily read it between the lines. *Verbum*, in contrast, expressly takes up the question (pp. 208–13), and shows how in Thomas 'analogy is transcended and we are confronted with the mystery' (p. 208).

28   Studied in Lonergan's unpublished notes, *De scientia atque voluntate Dei* (cap. 12), issued as class notes for his course 'De praedestinatione' at Regis College, Toronto, spring term, 1950.

29   *Summa Theologiae* Ia, q. 85, a. 3 c.: 'oportet considerare, quod intellectus noster de potentia in actum procedit . . .'.

30   He hopes, for example, to construct 'an *a priori* scheme of such generality that there can be no tendency to do violence to the data for the sake of maintaining the scheme', and to do so 'solely from a consideration of the nature of human speculation on a given subject': 'The *Gratia Operans* dissertation' (see note 16 above), p. 12.

31   B. Lonergan, '*Insight* revisited' in *A Second Collection*, pp. 266–7. See also *Caring*, pp. 51, 98.

32   The study was first published in five articles, spread over the years 1946–49, in *Theological Studies* 7, 8, and 10. They were published at Notre Dame in book form, with some editorial changes, by D. Burrell (see note 12 above); a year later this book was published with the correction of some misprints, in London; meanwhile, a French translation with its own differences, 'La notion de verbe dans les écrits de saint Thomas d'Aquin', had appeared in *Archives de Philosophie* 26–28 (1963–65) and was soon published under that title as a book (Paris, 1966). Both English and French books carry a new 'Introduction' by Lonergan, pp. vii–xv.

33   There are useful summaries of this main point in *Verbum*, pp. 47–8, 141–2, 183–7.

34   Ibid., pp. 33–4.

35   Ibid., pp. 45–6; see also pp. 97–8. The book devotes most of chapters 3–4 to metaphysics, after two chapters on the psychology of cognitional process.

36   *Caring*, p. 68.
37   B. Lonergan, 'Theology and understanding' in *Collection*, ed. F.E. Crowe and R. Doran (2nd edn; *Collected Works of Bernard Lonergan* 4; Toronto, 1988), p. 127.
38   B. Lonergan, 'Isomorphism of Thomist and scientific thought', ibid., p. 141; the Epilogue of *Verbum* begins and ends (pp. 215, 220) with discussion of the Leonine motto.
39   B. Lonergan, 'The future of Thomism' in *A Second Collection*, p. 44.
40   Ibid., pp. 47-9 (on classical Thomism), pp. 49-52 (on Thomism for tomorrow).
41   B. Lonergan, 'Isomorphism . . .', *Collection*, p. 133.
42   B. Lonergan, 'Aquinas today: tradition and innovation' in *A Third Collection*, ed. F.E. Crowe (New York/London, 1985), pp. 51-3.
43   See note 6 above.
44   B. Lonergan, *Philosophy of God, and Theology: The Relationship between Philosophy of God and the Functional Specialty, Systematics* (St Michael's Lectures, Gonzaga University, Spokane, 1972; London/Philadelphia, 1973), pp. 6-8.

3

The level of the times (I): *Insight*

The Preface Lonergan wrote in 1953 for *Insight* was not published with the book, but it appeared 30-odd years later with the story of the way it was discarded. It is worth retrieving as a whole, but one line is especially significant, for it links his return in *Insight* with the bright dreams of the 1930s, spanning the eleven years of his great withdrawal; 'if I may borrow a phrase from Ortega y Gasset', he wrote, 'one has to strive to mount to the level of one's time'.[1] To 'mount to the level of one's time'—that single luminous phrase describes, as well as any I know, the force that had driven Lonergan in his youth, was building up in his long apprenticeship to Thomas, is operative now in *Insight*, and will continue its dominance through the remaining 30 years of his writing career.

This was his concern in the 1935 letter to Henry Keane; it was the concern that guided his study of the *vetera* in Thomas Aquinas; it is his concern now as he begins work on the *nova*, and writes his great work, *Insight: A Study of Human Understanding*. We shall struggle to say something coherent on the content of that book and the purpose internal to it, but the remote controlling context is simplicity itself: Catholic thought is seven centuries behind the times, it must take a giant leap forward—*un balzo innanzi*, as Pope John would call it in the early days of the Second Vatican Council.[2] There is an important corrective here to the view that Lonergan was an intellectual recluse; on the contrary, he was what he came to see in Plato, not pure intellect but a reformer concerned with social decline.

One does not, however, mount to the level of the times in a series of ski-lifts; and even when there is a giant *balzo innanzi*, the way has been explored and prepared by a deal of steady footslogging. Much of Lonergan's journey was slogging too, and we hardly arrive at the goal with him except by sharing in the journey. Our sharing, however, has to be limited to the transitions that mark stages, heights where we may pause for a panorama.

I find it convenient to assign two stages to Lonergan's climb to the twentieth century: first, the writing of *Insight*, which I regard as coming to grips on one side with the empirical gains of the scientific revolution, and on the other with the critical philosophy of Immanuel Kant; and secondly, experiments in theological method, where he came to grips with the new human sciences and their concern for meaning and value, as well as with the questions the new historical consciousness was raising for Catholic truth—he had to relate all this to the systematic theology that was his arena of struggle during the 25 years he taught theology 'under impossible conditions'. That second stage will be the object of our study in Chapters 4 and 5.

About to begin now the present chapter on Lonergan's longest and most difficult work, I think of the reply he would sometimes give when explanation had failed to get a point across to an importunate questioner, 'Read *Insight*'. Or, softening somewhat, 'Read chapter 11 of *Insight*'. I would like to find some similar escape, and indeed believe my best contribution may lie in setting forth the context and purpose, the problematic and genesis of the work, rather than its content. Still, one cannot contract to write a book on Lonergan without some overview of his masterpiece, so I start with a brief survey of the contents of *Insight*, then deal more at length with questions of origin and genesis which easier access to the sources may help me to illuminate, and, finally, try to locate the book in its ongoing context.

THE CONTENTS OF *INSIGHT*: AN OVERVIEW

The book sets out to study the same insight into phantasm that the *verbum* articles had discovered, but to study it now in itself and in its implications, detached from its historical appearance in Aristotle and Thomas Aquinas. Chapter 1 finds illustrations of the act in the more static field of mathematics, chapters 2 to 5 in the more dynamic field of the empirical sciences, chapters 6 to 7 in the everyday world of common sense, and chapter 8 in the world of things that is shared by science and common sense.[3] These eight chapters regard insight, or understanding, in its direct form of insight into data or presentations, into phantasm or image; but besides the direct form there is the reflective form that is at the origin of judgement, and so chapters 9 to 10 consider that phase of cognitional activity. The two levels were distinguished already in *Verbum* (chapters 1 and 2), but there the controlling phrase was the *duplex operatio* of Thomas, one operation regarding quiddities, the other regarding judgement; now the controlling phrase is 'levels of consciousness'.

A useful clarification may be inserted here. Reflective insight is not to be confused with inverse insight: inverse insight belongs with direct insight on the second level of consciousness, and both regard intelligibility—direct to discover its presence, inverse to discover its absence; but reflective insight is on the third level of consciousness.

The first ten chapters, then, study Insight as Activity, and are so entitled. They are followed by a second part, likewise of ten chapters: Insight as Knowledge. The two parts answer two questions and are related the way the two questions are: 'The first part deals with the question, What is happening when we are knowing? The second moves to the question, What is known when that is happening?'[4] This, of course, gives his view when he had completed the book and was writing the Introduction; on starting the book some years before, he did not have the pattern quite so clear, and several years later he would advance to still another view, seeing the book now as answering three questions.[5]

The content of Insight as Knowledge has no fixed boundaries; in contrast the first part of the book, Insight as Activity, has a certain stability determined by the structure of cognitional activity. One may illustrate the activity in a million ways, and Lonergan provides copious examples, but whenever one comes to know something, one has observed data, formulated an idea on their explanation or meaning, and taken steps to verify that idea—thus the three recurring steps in cognitional process, fixed in their basic mutual relations, but flexible in their occurrence and variety of application. What one comes to know, however—Insight as Knowledge—has no boundaries, nor is it subject to easy schematization. In a general sense it is reality, known in a general way in metaphysics. But the reality subdivides in alarming fashion, as the multiplication of departments in a university testifies.

Thus, the second part of the book finds that the elements of metaphysics lead into the history of human thought, its varieties of expression, the problem of interpreting those expressions (ch. 17).

The consistency that some dynamism, deep in our interior, demands between our knowing and our doing, leads to the question of the possibility of ethics (ch. 18). The question of what may be beyond the area of our finite knowing and doing rises now in virtue of the same dynamism, for as a questioning dynamism it knows no boundaries and suppresses no question whatever (ch. 19). The question of the 'beyond', if answered with an affirmation of One who is wise and good at the origin of our universe, leads at once to the question what that One who is wise and good, and at the origin of our universe, may be expected to do about the evil in our universe (ch. 20).[6]

So much for an overview of the book, the rough summary that one might derive very simply from the table of contents. But this makes it look like a book in which what counts is the content to be communicated, in particular a book of philosophy, written with the aim of communicating a basic philosophic content. That is not the case at all in *Insight*. I have no doubt that one could distil a philosophy from the book, but its internal aim is altogether different. So Lonergan declares in the first paragraph of his Introduction, and his word of caution is worth repeating:

> The aim of the present work may be bracketed by a series of disjunctions. In the first place, the question is not whether knowledge exists but what precisely is its nature. Secondly, while the content of the known cannot be disregarded, still it is to be treated only in the schematic and incomplete fashion needed to provide a discriminant or determinant of cognitive acts. Thirdly, the aim is not to set forth a list of the abstract properties of human knowledge but to assist the reader in effecting a personal appropriation of the concrete, dynamic structure immanent and recurrently operative in his own cognitional activities. Fourthly, such an appropriation can occur only gradually, and so there will be offered, not a sudden account of the whole of the structure, but a slow assembly of its elements, relations, alternatives, and implications. Fifthly, the order of the assembly is governed, not by abstract considerations of logical or metaphysical priority, but by concrete motives of pedagogical efficacy.[7]

From the 'table of contents' I provided, and this long quotation from Lonergan on the aim internal to the book, the reader will have some idea—Newman's notional apprehension at least—of what the book 'says'. What can I add on this point? There are literally hundreds of ideas in *Insight* calling each for its own monograph. I cannot provide all the doctoral dissertations needed to study them, and even if I could and did, I would have missed the point of the book. I believe I can best employ the space given me by turning to matters at one remove from the content, and in some measure external to it.

WHAT IS LONERGAN UP TO IN *INSIGHT*?

I begin with Lonergan's purpose in the context of his lifework. His five disjunctions pin down the aim internal to the book, but the question can be asked on the broader view of his general orientation, What was he doing here? Why did he write the book at all? As he himself once asked of Lévi-Strauss,[8] what was he up to?

We know from his own later account that he set out to write a book on theological method, and rounded it off at the level of philosophy when called to Rome in 1953.[9] But where was he going with his theological method, and how would a book on insight be a step on the way? There was, of course, the scandal of disputed questions,[10] a symptom of the degree to which Catholic thought had fallen behind the times, but what course were the 'times' and human thought taking, and what precise place in that history did he expect *Insight* to occupy?

One way to approach this question is to put it in terms of adversaries. In his *verbum* articles he had conceptualism in his sights throughout; was there a corresponding adversary in *Insight*? or, at least, a partner in dialogue? I suggest, with inevitable oversimplification, that he had two partners, and that the two are linked in themselves and in his way of dealing with them. They are the overwhelming advances of the scientific revolution, and the critical turn taken in the philosophy of Kant. The two are linked in themselves, in that Kant philosophized in the context of Newton and the scientific revolution. They are likewise linked in Lonergan's treatment of them, in that they represent two areas in which Catholic thought had noticeably fallen behind, and his stated aim was to bring Catholic thinking up to date; specifically, they would be his partners in dialogue on the question, so basic to Lonergan, of cognitional theory. The book abounds in weighty discussions of common sense and philosophies, and the discussions are not just marginal, but neither are they, I believe, at the focus of his attention.

I must digress here to attend briefly to the objection, superficial but curiously widespread, that Lonergan's cognitional theory is based on, and applies to, science alone. Science is his exhibit A, but he finds his cognitional theory also, and says so over and over again, in common sense, which has exactly the same basic structure as scientific knowledge, asks its questions in the same basic order, and answers them in virtue of the same basic dynamism 'immanent and recurrently operative' within us. He doesn't start his book with common sense, because data there are endless and hard to pinpoint, because extraneous questions so often intervene, because the criteria for common-sense judgements are hard to isolate, because common sense is oriented to the practical with little theoretic interest in its own procedures, and so on.[11]

Science, in contrast, provided him with the most exact, accessible, and clear-cut illustration of what human knowing is. Namely, attending to data; then, asking how they are to be explained and formulating an idea of a possible explanation; thirdly, asking whether the idea is correct—the conditioned proposition—and finding the evidence that turns the conditioned proposition into an unconditioned. The structure he had discovered in Thomas Aquinas emerged with new clarity and wider implications in modern science.[12] But science, in its more recent advances, had still further implications that took cognitional theorists beyond questions of structure into the area of epistemology. The unimaginable object of relativity and the unimaginable event of quantum mechanics confirmed Lonergan's definition of what the real is: not what one can look at, or what one can imagine, but what is, where 'what is' is what one can know through intelligent grasp and reasonable affirmation.

If I have understood Lonergan's dialogue with Kant and modern science, we are dealing exactly with the knowledge that Kant aspired to but proved in his critique to be unattainable, and that modern science has gone ahead and attained, even if only in probable judgements and with revisable results. For modern science, human knowing is definitely not 'taking a look'; rather the real object sought in the human cognitional quest is approached in a conditioned proposition, the conditions for fulfilment of which Kant did not manage to find. Lonergan's position on the virtually unconditioned as a constitutive factor in judgement, and therefore in knowing, met that difficulty head on. Among all the differences between his cognitional theory and Kant's he seems to regard this as the crucial one; there is the battle line, and he stands or falls with his position on the virtually unconditioned.

With this we are at the heart of the critical problem. Everyone sees that, of course. But what Lonergan saw—and it is testimony to the depth of his thought that he saw it—was, first, that the discovery of insight has the most serious implications for epistemology and, next, that modern science is a powerful aid to the solution of that problem.

The object of insight was the intelligible in the imagined, but the intelligible goes beyond the imagined, and no amount of looking or imagining will of itself verify the intelligible. Once that point was gained, the critical problem loomed as a grave threat for philosophers. The comfortable way of 'taking a look' is no longer enough. But if a look is not enough, where do we find the real? If we are not content with an ideal world, we must face the critical problem, as the *verbum* study had already made clear:

> For the materialist, the real is what he knows before he understands or thinks: it is the sensitively integrated object that is reality for a dog; it is the sure and firm-set earth on which I tread, which is so reassuring to the sense of reality; and on that showing, intellect does not penetrate to the inwardness of things but is a merely subjective, if highly useful, principle of activity. To the Pythagoreans the discovery of harmonic ratios revealed that numbers and their proportions, though primarily ideas, nonetheless have a role in making things what they are . . . Socratic interest in definition reinforced this tendency, but the Platonist sought the reality known by thought, not in this world, but in another. Aristotle's basic thesis was the objective reality of what is known by understanding.[13]

Aristotle's philosophic position must be validated on philosophic grounds, but *Insight* finds a powerful ally in modern science: 'it was left to twentieth-century physicists to envisage the possibility that the objects of their science were to be reached only by severing the umbilical cord that tied them to the maternal imagination of man'.[14]

It is the Halifax lectures on the book one year after its publication that present the problem starkly: 'if you frankly acknowledge that intellect is intelligence, you discover that you have terrific problems in epistemology'.[15] But what on earth does he mean? What else could intellect be but intelligence? Twice in the discussion following the lectures this question was raised.[16] Lonergan's three-levelled cognitional structure, where on the second level insight is the source of concepts, and on the third level reflective grasp of the unconditioned is the source of judgement, provides the answer. Intellect as intelligence is intellect as understanding; it means that to verify the idea you need more than a look at the data; you need the virtually unconditioned.

If this centre holds, it may add unexpected strength to the wings. It means, for example, that metaphysics is no more difficult for the human mind than is a verified empirical science; it means that knowledge of God's existence is as natural to human knowing as knowledge of special relativity is. The real is being, or in language that has more resonance, the real is that which is. 'Is' is the easiest word in the English language to use, for we are all natural, if latent, metaphysicians. But, if 'is' is not known by taking a look, if there is not an 'isness' to be understood as triangularity can be understood, then 'is' becomes the hardest of all words to justify—so, while some philosophers are tempted to jettison metaphysics for language studies, Lonergan turns to a virtually unconditioned that is a constitutive factor in human knowing.

It would be naive to expect all this to 'take' (as we used to say about vaccinations) on the mere basis of argument. It will not 'take', it will not, as an argument, produce assent. As an argument it is just words. If the words and their sequence could be tidied up to the satisfaction of a logician, one might run them through a logic-machine and get the answers I have set forth. But who tidied them up, who put them in the logic-machine, with what meaning, and by what authority? The best syllogism in the world is no better than its premises, and the premises have to be affirmed in a human mind in order to 'take'. Thus *Insight* remains forever an invitation. There is no question that it states the author's position, and states what he regards as the true position; but it will never truly and rationally be anyone else's position except through that person's own activity in coming to grips with the cognitional process that is native to all of us. Lonergan saw his book as pedagogical, but perhaps what is pedagogy in him becomes pedantry in his followers; certainly, I should not continue to argue what I have just said cannot be communicated by argument. I continue, then, to skirt the issues raised by the book, and will instead contribute what I can from external data.

THE GENESIS OF *INSIGHT* (1): SOURCES FOR A HISTORY

Continuing my backward journey through the thrust and purpose of the book, I come to the history of its composition, Lonergan's own road of discovery, a kind of progress report on his year-by-year development. I personally find this history helpful for understanding how he came to write what he did in the way he did, helpful too for understanding his point of arrival, and in any case more interesting than a second-hand exposition of his ideas. I should, however, remark at once that the history involves both previous and subsequent periods. As he had learned by the time he wrote *Method in Theology*, there is an ongoing context of interpretation, which 'necessitates a distinction between prior and subsequent context'.[17] But, first, the prior stage: the genesis of *Insight*.

We remember that Lonergan, reminiscing 60 years later, recalled that as a young boy he had already glimpsed the centrality of understanding; we remember too that his first semi-published article was already an exercise in insight into phantasm and prepared him for the discovery of a similar exercise in Aristotle and Thomas Aquinas, but that he turned somewhat away during the 1930s from this promising beginning, to engage instead the questions of history represented by Hegel and Marx.

Still, the magnetic pole of understanding maintained its attraction. He had noticed the prominence of *intelligere* (understanding) in Augustine;[18] likewise, Augustine's lack of interest in universals, 'though the knowledge of universals was supposed to be the be-all and end-all of science'.[19] So he came to write the *verbum* articles, which he regarded as 'the historical side', and *Insight*, 'the theoretical side' of a single question.[20]

Though actual writing of the book started only in 1949—'I worked at *Insight* from 1949 to 1953'[21]—Lonergan regarded the 1945–46 lectures on 'Thought and reality' as the real beginning in the sense that they provided the proof that he had a book in the making.[22] He seems to have been curiously diffident on this point, as appears from his repeated reference to the perseverance of his class throughout that year of lectures and to the girl who thumped the table exclaiming 'I've got it'.[23] An account of the genesis of the book must, I think, begin with those lectures as a catalytic agent in Lonergan's decision and not just as a preliminary sketch of his idea.

It is possible now to trace Lonergan's steps from 1945 to 1955 through the following documents: notes on the lectures 'Thought and reality', Thomas More Institute, Montreal, 1945–46; notes on another set of lectures there in 1951, this time called 'Intelligence and reality' (a significant change); notes on lectures in 1952–53, given while he was writing the book, at Regis College, Toronto; contemporary letters and later interviews that reveal stages of the work in progress; finally, the text itself: his own typescript with the innumerable rewrites that it reveals, the revisions he made on the good copy his typists supplied, the further very extensive revisions made when he received the reports of the publisher's readers, revisions made at the proof stage. To all this we will later add his interpretation of his work as he saw it in the ongoing context of the years.[24]

THE GENESIS OF *INSIGHT* (2): EXPLORATORY LECTURES

For the 1945–46 lectures on 'Thought and reality', we have student notes taken by J. Martin O'Hara, scribbled in haste but clear and coherent; also Lonergan's own notes discovered after his death, though they are deficient on the second half of the course; and, thirdly, a kind of syllabus for examinations at the year's end.[25] From these it is possible to track the two parts indicated in the title—at least the transition from one to the other is clear. 'Thought' seems to have three subdivisions, which I would designate: what science is, the structure of reality (its metaphysical constituents), and cognitional theory. 'Reality' also seems to have three parts: truth, being, and the problem of transition from subjective necessity to the certainty of objective truth. One senses a certain lack of order, and we remember his remark in the *verbum* articles, on attempting 'in a variety of ways' which he found 'unmanageable' to make metaphysics precede psychology; these lectures may be one of those unmanageable ways.[26]

Some points of detail are quite interesting. For example, he has four types of the act of understanding: direct, judicial, contemplative, and methodical—the first two are the familiar pair, but what became of the latter two? Again, he has a cross dialectic, similar to what he will later call the canon of operations: the sequence of data, insight, hypothesis, deduction, verification, repeated again with a new datum, a new insight, and so on. There is also an upward dialectic—in a favourite metaphor, the circular staircase—which involves both a shift in the meaning of the terms and an analogy of proportion between earlier and later stages. Then there is the intriguing term, 'dummy insight', which continues to crop up years later and is identified here with the x that we would know if we achieved insight.[27]

Very interesting too are his notes on the originality of St Thomas (possibly not used in the course, since they do not appear in the O'Hara report); Lonergan sees this originality most clearly in

Thomas's development: development on the moral impotence of the sinner, on free will, on the causal certitude of providence, on actual grace, on the natural appetite for beatitude, and on the *verbum mentis*, the inner word. There follows a discussion of three historical movements: the Aristotelian reconciliation of sense and concept; the move of Christian thinkers to truth (Augustine and others); and, thirdly, the problem of truth: we cannot compare the real object as known with the real object as unknown, so how can we know they equate? Here Lonergan sketches an epistemology that will be amplified in the second of the *verbum* articles.[28]

Five years later, in the spring of 1951, Lonergan repeated his lectures at Thomas More Institute, this time giving them the title 'Intelligence and reality', and providing semi-official notes for his students.[29] The lectures begin with the act of understanding, then go into such questions as higher viewpoint, explanatory and heuristic abstraction, empirical method with its two phases: classical and statistical, then go on to things (there is no special lecture on common sense), and so to judgement. There follow pages on the pure desire to know, on radical intellectual conversion, on the notion of being, and on the notion of objectivity. There is a helpful page on the history of confrontationism—the view that knowing is 'taking a look'—and the topics are rounded off with the categories of proportionate being. The lectures conclude with more general questions on the starting point of philosophy, and the question, What good is philosophy?

These lectures are naturally much closer to the book. There is the same description and analysis of the act of insight, and the same position on its central role; the same position also on the three levels of cognitional process and their interrelations; and again on the virtually unconditioned and the resulting judgement. Here, as in the book, the real question is not whether there is knowledge, but what knowledge is, and the myth to overcome in both lectures and book is that knowing consists in 'taking a look'.

Interesting are the points sketched here that look ahead rather to *Method* than to *Insight*: the need for a radical intellectual conversion[30] (remarkable that *Insight* from beginning to end is an exercise in radical intellectual conversion, yet never says so, and the book's only mention of 'conversion' is in reference to Augustine's), and subjective achievement as the root of objectivity.[31] It is especially remarkable that the last paragraph of the notes is on the insufficiency of philosophy, and they end with a reference to the new love 'poured forth in your hearts by the Holy Spirit who is given you'—

the text from Romans 5 that is so characteristic of the later Lonergan. These points help establish the continuity of *Insight* and *Method*; the lectures were given, we remember, before Lonergan knew he would be forced to divide his project into those two works.

Even more interesting are the developments from the 1951 lectures to the book. The six canons of empirical method (ch. 3 in the book) have a modest forerunner in the lectures with their two 'basic principles': the principle of exclusion, corresponding to the canon of selection; and the principle of relevance, which does touch *Insight*'s canon of relevance but is closer to the canon of parsimony.[32] Again, in the lectures the notion of being divides into pure and composite: the first is the unrestricted desire, the second adds questions, answers, and so on.[33]

Some changes from lectures to book seem rather a cautious step back than a forward development. In *Insight* we have six metaphysical elements: central potency, form, and act; and conjugate potency, form, and act. But in the lectures we have nine elements (called there terminal categories of proportionate being): besides the central three (called there substantial) and the conjugate three, we have group potency, group form, group act. Not only does Lonergan list this with the other two sets, he gives the three elements of this set the same permanence in any metaphysics as he does the other six.

What became of them in *Insight*? They are there in chapter 15, but not expressly as three distinct metaphysical elements. For, as defined in the lectures, group form is emergent probability; group act is the functioning, the totality of occurrences as actually realized; group potency is the 'minimum set of substantial and conjugate potencies, forms, and acts that has to be postulated to account for functioning through emergent probability'.[34] Now these are found in chapter 15 of the book, and found in their proper place: after two sections on the six elements of metaphysics, we have a section on explanatory genera and species; the rest of the chapter, in fact, is concerned with development and genetic method. Further, in his concluding summary, after running through the six elements again, Lonergan continues:

> From the structural unification of the methods by generalized emergent probability, there follow the structural account of the explanatory genera and species and the immanent order of the universe of proportionate being. Such are the elements of metaphysics.[35]

'Such' evidently includes the quoted sentence along with the six numbered elements. In other words, to the static consideration of traditional metaphysics, there is added the dynamic consideration of a developing world order. Why Lonergan dropped his terminology of group potency, form, act is a good question; but I suspect he did it simply for pedagogical and tactical reasons.

THE GENESIS OF *INSIGHT* (3): ACTUAL COMPOSITION

Lonergan's third set of lectures (Regis College, Toronto, 1952–53) are very close to the book as far as they go,[36] so we may leave them aside and turn to another approach to his developing ideas: the data on the actual order of writing and composition. This we find in the extant manuscripts,[37] and in letters, interviews, and recollections.

The first 'unit' prepared for the typist, on Lonergan's own testimony,[38] comprised the chapters later numbered 9 to 13: judgement, reflective understanding, self-affirmation, being, objectivity. The manuscript evidence agrees, for his typing here is single-spaced throughout those five chapters. This is the case also throughout chapters 1 to 5, and in the first nine pages of chapter 6; then, oddly, but the result perhaps of taking pity on his typists,[39] he changed to double-spacing, a practice which continues to the end of chapter 8, and is renewed from chapter 14 to the end of the book. It is altogether unlikely that he would inflict single-spacing on his typists after starting with double, so we have a good clue here to the general order of his writing: first, chapters 9 to 13, then 1 to 8, and finally 14 to 20 and the Epilogue. The Preface, of course, was written last of all,[40] recording the dates of actual writing, 'June 1949 to September 1953'.[41]

Did Lonergan have an overall plan of the whole and its parts as he began writing in 1949? Maybe detective work on his papers, letters and interviews will reveal such a design. But, however he conceived the whole work, it seems at least that chapters 1 to 13 would have formed a unit. That is certainly the way he saw them twenty years later, when he spoke as follows:

> With chapter thirteen the book could end. The first eight chapters explore human understanding. The next five reveal how correct understanding can be discerned . . . However . . . if I went no further, my work would be regarded as . . . incapable of grounding a metaphysics . . . A metaphysics could be

70

possible and yet an ethics impossible. An ethics could be possible and yet arguments for God's existence impossible. In that fashion seven more chapters and an epilogue came to be written.[42]

The content of those additional chapters, and the way they fit into what may have been his overall plan, are intriguing questions with plenty of scope for further detective work. It is clear that his general purpose was to write on theological method; it is also clear that late in 1952 he decided that he must 'round off' his work before going to Rome; it seems that those last seven chapters were the rounding off, and that they were written in the seven or eight months from December 1952 to July 1953.

There is a basis for this in his own testimony:

I worked at *Insight* from 1949 to 1953. During the first three years my intention was an exploration of methods generally in preparation for a study of the method of theology. But in 1952 it became clear that I was due to start teaching at the Gregorian University in Rome in 1953, so I changed my plan and decided to round off what I had done and publish it . . .'[43]

This decision was taken only in the fall of 1952, for a letter written in December speaks of his conversations with Paul Dezza and Charles Boyer as a factor in his decision, and Boyer's visit to Regis College occurred in late September.[44]

This same letter fills a gap in our history with its clear account of the state of the work at that time:

About 12 chapters done. About 6 chapters to go . . . Topics: insight in maths, empirical science, common sense, knowing things, judgment; objectivity of insight; nature of metaphysics; God; dialectic of individual consciousness (Freud) of community (Marx) of objectivity (philosophies), of religion. Had hoped to include theology, but impossible now that I am going to Rome in September.[45]

The twelve 'chapters done' would very probably be chapters 1 to 13 of the book, since the present chapters 6 and 7 were originally just one. But the utterly mind-boggling fact lies in *what was not yet done*: chapters 14 to 20. Those extraordinary chapters were written—at white heat, surely—between December 1952 and August 1953, for I read the manuscript (not the Preface, and possibly not the Introduction) in early August, when the final sections had already been returned by the typists.

The headings themselves of the December letter, in their difference from the published work, show that the work of 'rounding off' had not yet been definitively thought out. Material in the Lonergan Archives confirms this. A table of contents among his scattered papers lists eight chapters, numbered 11 to 18, in the second part of the book; they are entitled: 'Self-affirmation', 'The notion of being', 'The notion of objectivity', 'The dialectic of philosophy', 'Elements of metaphysics', 'Elements of ethics', 'Elements of natural theology', 'The structure of history'.[46] This is surely intermediate between the December letter and the book; it shows Lonergan still thinking out his plan, but he is at least close to the book now; even 'the structure of history', which does not appear in the book and might seem to have been discarded, turns out to be the present chapter 20 on special transcendent knowledge.[47]

The manuscripts reveal specific developments of interest.[48] What in December he had called 'The dialectic of philosophy' became the present chapter 14, 'The method of metaphysics'. This did not change the content: some time after getting the typist's copy, Lonergan simply crossed out one title and wrote in the other. A more surprising change follows chapter 15 ('The elements of metaphysics'): in Lonergan's manuscript, the present chapter 16, the first two sections of chapter 17 ('Metaphysics, mystery, and myth'; 'The notion of truth'), and the first two sections of chapter 18 ('The notion of the good'; 'The notion of freedom') were all composed under the running head, 'The deepening of metaphysics'. Evidently Lonergan found the 'depths' of metaphysics to require diversification, so he divided his one long chapter (a book in itself, surely) into three, gave its own title to chapter 16 ('Metaphysics as science'), and added further sections to give us the present chapter 17 ('Metaphysics as dialectic') and chapter 18 ('The possibility of ethics'). The original plan of including them in a single chapter provides, among other insights, a useful clue to the continuity he saw between metaphysics and ethics. A final note: there was to be a chapter on God, and this is the running head for the first four sections of what is now chapter 19; presumably, as Lonergan began the fifth section ('The idea of being'), he formed the idea of substituting 'Special transcendent knowledge' for 'The structure of history', and so changed the title of the chapter from 'God' to 'General transcendent knowledge'.

INSIGHT: THE ONGOING CONTEXT

The amount of space I gave to the genesis of *Insight*, compared to the few paragraphs I wrote in outline of its content, is justified, I hope, as giving somewhat easier access to what the book is all about than would be—what is impossible here in any case—a detailed exposition of its ideas and positions. It is further justified as a preparation for the last section of this chapter: the later history of the book, not as an account of its editions, reprints, sales, and reviews,[49] but as an ongoing history of its ideas.

The previous section ended with samples of the changes Lonergan kept making in his book as he worked it out. The changes may have had simply tactical and pedagogical purposes, or they may signify deepening understanding, or it is quite possible that they exhibit changes, more or less marked, in his ideas or positions. Whatever the explanation, one conclusion is clear: *Insight*, though a monumental piece of work, is not a finished product. I would go further, and say that it never will be finished, and indeed never should be finished. In approach it is a long dialogue with readers inviting them to self-appropriation, and it is no more likely that the dialogue will peter out than that self-appropriation will be permanently achieved by anyone, Lonergan himself included. As for content, I repeat my earlier remark, that while Part One of the book may reveal a fixed structure, Part Two is wide open to all the possibilities of emergent probability in the material universe, developing intelligence in the human, and divine intervention in the total scheme of things.

Thirty-four years have passed since *Insight* was published. Whole great areas of established approaches and positions in academe continue to ignore it, but among the unattached students of new generations interest grows steadily, the book's place in the history of thought seems secure, and dialogue with a solid core of thinkers continues. The social aspect of Lonergan's work, his youthful aspiration to speak to the needs of the times on the level of the times, this is slowly moving to realization.

Every social being is individual too. Can we then speak also of Lonergan's ongoing dialogue with himself? Certainly he did not cease developing in September 1953. He was scarcely installed in Rome when he rewrote some pages of his manuscript;[50] on receiving the reports of the Longmans readers in 1954 he rewrote some 70 pages;[51] in April 1958 he rewrote several passages for the second revised edition;[52] his copy of the 1970 edition in the Lonergan Archives is annotated in what appear to be further reflections on the ideas and positions of the book.[53] Then, for years afterwards, there were numerous courses and single lectures on the book, some published, some on tape, some in transcript.[54]

It is a profitable exercise to compare the book with his lectures on it and with other later publications that continue his restless search for deeper understanding; one might note the advances, for example, on the question of probability in the lectures at Saint Mary's University, Halifax, in 1958.[55] Lonergan was thinking too of a book that would systematize *Insight*,[56] though surely not to harden its positions into an abstract system. Some years later he substitutes, for the two questions of his Introduction, three linked questions that he considers the book to answer: 'What am I doing when I am knowing? Why is doing that knowing? What do I know when I do it?'[57] He had already distinguished sciences of the object from sciences of objectification,[58] and this enables us to see the three questions as yielding a science of the subject in the early chapters, a science of the object in the later chapters, and a science of objectification in the middle chapters. Then, in *Method in Theology*, he remarks on the relation that positions of that work bear to the less differentiated positions of *Insight*.[59] Later still, he offers his own critique of *Insight*'s famous chapter 19 and the proof of God's existence.[60] The last formal statement he made on *Insight*, so far as I know, was a response in 1977 to a Harper & Row book editor who had requested material for a blurb for a new reprint.[61] His answers are succinct, precisely tailored to the space provided on the questionnaire. To the third question, 'For whom have you written this book?', he replied as follows:

> For anyone, I should say, who really wishes to think things through. Thinking things through can hardly omit thinking itself through, that is, studying the mind that does the thinking. But initially the human mind is just a black box: the input we know is sensation; the output we know is talk. But what precisely goes on in between to transform the input into the output? That seems to be the cardinal question: cardinal, because so much depends upon its solution; question, because down the millennia consensus has not been obtained.

To the fourth question, 'What sets this book apart from others now available?', his answer was this:

> It is an offer to share, an invitation to participate. One really gets to know the human mind through attention, not to objects,

but to one's own conscious operation with respect to objects. Just as in some types of therapy one learns to advert to, name, recognize, identify one's previously submerged feelings, so in this book one is invited to discover in oneself precisely experienced operations and the dynamism that leads from one type to another. In the measure that discovery is made, one will find oneself in possession of the referents of a basic set of terms and relations. That possession will lead to a self-understanding based on the fact of understanding one's self.

And to the fifth, 'What might the reader experience in pursuing this book?', he wrote this answer:

Examples of insight are drawn from mathematics, physics, common sense, and philosophy. The temptation [of the reader] will be to think of such objects and neglect his own operations with respect to the objects. This is missing the whole point. The various objects are mentioned only to invite the reader to heighten his consciousness of the operations he is performing in dealing with the objects. Once this pitfall is avoided, and the avoidance is not easy, there can emerge a growing illumination that leads the reader no longer to need Lonergan because he has found out for himself and can work on his own.

For Lonergan himself to 'work on his own' owed a great deal to working on another, the eleven years he spent 'reaching up to the mind of Aquinas'; for some of us it is a matter of reaching up to the mind of Lonergan and trying to discover what dynamism was at work in him as he advanced from position to position. I remember a passage from the *verbum* study that tells us, as well as any other, what dynamism was at work as he wrote *Insight*; it will serve to close this chapter.[62]

The specific drive of our nature is to understand, and indeed to understand everything, neither confusing the trees with the forest nor content to contemplate the forest without seeing all the trees. For the spirit of inquiry within us never calls a halt, never can be satisfied, until our intellects, united to God as body to soul, know *ipsum intelligere* and through that vision, though then knowing aught else is a trifle, contemplate the universe as well.

Notes

1   B. Lonergan, 'The original Preface of *Insight*', *Method: Journal of Lonergan Studies* 3/1 (March 1985), p. 4. I have told there the story of how, on the suggestion of T. Michael Longman in the summer of 1954, Lonergan came to write another Preface: F. Crowe, 'A note on the Prefaces of *Insight*', ibid., pp. 1–3; the new one was somewhat longer, pp. ix–xv in *Insight: A Study of Human Understanding* (London/New York, 1957; revised students' edition, 1958). As far as I know, no one has studied the relation of Lonergan to the thought of Ortega y Gasset, which seems to extend beyond the brief quotation in the original Preface.

2   *Acta Apostolicae Sedis* 55 (1963), pp. 43–5.

3   In his answer, summer of 1977, to a questionnaire from John Loudon, book editor for Harper & Row, who had requested advertising material for a reprint of the book, Lonergan wrote 'Examples of insight are drawn from mathematics, physics, common sense, and philosophy'.

4   B. Lonergan, *Insight*, p. xxii.

5   B. Lonergan, 'Theories of inquiry: responses to a symposium' in *A Second Collection*, ed. W. Ryan and B. Tyrrell (London/Philadelphia, 1974/1975), p. 37: 'the procedure followed in *Insight* was to treat three linked questions: What am I doing when I am knowing? Why is doing that knowing? What do I know when I do it?'

6   A series of questions like this had a role in the actual writing, with Lonergan adding chapter to chapter as he went; see the quotation on pp. 70–1 above, and the references given in note 42 below.

7   B. Lonergan, *Insight*, p. xvii.

8   B. Lonergan, 'What is Claude Lévi-Strauss up to?', unpublished paper, York University, Toronto, November 1978.

9   B. Lonergan, '*Insight* revisited', p. 268.

10 B. Lonergan, *Method in Theology* (London/New York, 1972), p. 20: 'The scandal still continues that men, while they tend to agree on scientific questions, tend to disagree in the most outrageous fashion on basic philosophic issues'. See also *Insight*, p. xxvii. The point comes up repeatedly in Lonergan's writings; see 'The future of Thomism' in *A Second Collection*, p. 51: 'Without such a basis [in method] systematic theology will remain what it has been too often in the past, a morass of questions disputed endlessly and fruitlessly'.

11 During the Halifax lectures on *Insight* in 1958, Lonergan was asked directly whether the processes of experience, understanding, and judgement apply to common sense; he answered just as directly in the affirmative, and went on to give some of his reasons for starting his book with the more exact sciences; see *Understanding and Being: The Halifax Lectures on* Insight, ed. E. Morelli and M. Morelli (*Collected Works of Bernard Lonergan* 5; Toronto, 1990), pp. 304–6.

12 The relation of Thomism and science is studied in B. Lonergan, 'Isomorphism of Thomist and scientific thought' in *Collection*, ed. F. E. Crowe and R. M. Doran (2nd edn; *Collected Works of Bernard Lonergan* 4; Toronto, 1988), pp. 133–41.

13 B. Lonergan, *Verbum: Word and Idea in Aquinas*, ed. D. Burrell (Notre Dame/London, 1967/1968), p. 20 (my quotation corrects a misprint). ·

14 B. Lonergan, *Insight*, p. xxi.

15 B. Lonergan, *Understanding and Being*, p. 19.

16 Ibid., pp. 293-4, 350-2. See also the indexes under 'Critical', 'Epistemology'.

17 B. Lonergan, *Method in Theology*, p. 313.

18 B. Lonergan, '*Insight* revisited', p. 265. See also P. Lambert, C. Tansey and C. Going (eds), *Caring about Meaning: Patterns in the Life of Bernard Lonergan* (Montreal, 1982), pp. 22, 51.

19 *Caring*, p. 51.

20 B. Lonergan, 'Isomorphism of Thomist and scientific thought', p. 141.

21 See note 9 above. The original Preface is more precise: 'June 1949 to September 1953', *Method: Journal of Lonergan Studies* 3/1 (March 1985), p. 7; but the work was finished (except for the Preface and perhaps the Introduction) by early August.

22 B. Lonergan, '*Insight* revisited', p. 268; the importance of this appears in the way Lonergan repeated, in lectures and interviews, this 'proof' that he had a book.

23 Ibid. This part of the story was also related on different occasions.

24 There is some similarity between the 'moving viewpoint' with which he wrote the book (*Insight*, pp. xxiii-xxvi) and the ongoing context in which it is read, but the first is a pedagogical device, the second is a matter of the historicity of human thinking.

25 The 30 pages of Martin O'Hara's handwritten notes have been converted to typescript by Thomas V. Daly, and provided with an index (Lonergan Archives).

26 B. Lonergan, *Verbum*, p. 46. This first article was published in the September 1946 issue of *Theological Studies*; it must have gone to the editor at the latest in the spring, around the time Lonergan was finishing the lectures 'Thought and reality'.

27 See pp. 10 and 11 of Lonergan's own notes, and p. 9 of the O'Hara notes.

28 The originality of Thomas and the three historical movements: pp. 15-17 of Lonergan's notes; epistemology: ibid., p. 17, but more at length in the O'Hara notes, pp. 26-30.

29 The lectures began 26 March 1951, and ran till May. Lonergan provided 29 pages of notes; a notation on the first page (not in his hand), '1950-51 *Intelligence and Reality*', led to the error that the lectures spanned the academic year; probably the course did, but Lonergan's lectures came at the end.

30 Lonergan's notes, p. 14; *Insight*'s reference to Augustine's conversion: p. xxi.

31 Lonergan's notes, p. 29.

32 Ibid., p. 7.

33 Ibid., pp. 15-16.

34 Ibid., p. 24.

35 B. Lonergan, *Insight*, p. 486.

36   The late Thomas Hanley was then a theology student at Regis College, followed the course, and took 78 pages (half legal-size) of reliable notes, checked with his classmates (Lonergan Archives).

37   The pages of Lonergan's own typescript are filled with crossed-out lines and paragraphs, and even these pages are a residue from hundreds he scrapped (he left these behind when he went to Rome in September 1953, but the new occupant of his room did not save them); Lonergan did, however, keep scattered pages, sketches of a table of contents, and so on. The professionally done typescript also has its share of revisions, and the revising continued up to and including the galleys stage; the galleys with his corrections are in the Archives with the manuscripts.

38   B. Lonergan, letter to F. E. Crowe, 24 September 1954; the context was the question of retyping some rather dim pages of the carbon copy: 'the poorest part is what was done first namely chapters 9–13'.

39   Most of the typing was volunteer work by Beatrice Kelly (later White), who had followed Lonergan's lectures at Thomas More Institute, Montreal, was professionally experienced in typing scientific manuscripts, and so could handle, better than most, the first five chapters of the book; at least two chapters (18 and 19) were typed by Bernard's loyal brother, Gregory.

40   B. Lonergan, *Caring*, p. 43.

41   See notes 1, 9 above.

42   B. Lonergan, '*Insight* revisited', p. 275. See too 'An interview with Fr. Bernard Lonergan, S. J.' in *A Second Collection*, p. 222; also *Caring*, pp. 70, 229.

43   B. Lonergan, '*Insight* revisited', p. 268.

44   *The News-Letter: Upper Canada Province* [of Jesuits] 27/7 (September 1952), p. 1; 27/8 (October 1953), p. 1: 'Fr. Boyer visited the Seminary, September 26–28'.

45   B. Lonergan, letter to F. E. Crowe, 23 December 1952.

46   Papers in the Lonergan Archives, Batch IV, File 4a (as catalogued by Philip McShane). Various pages in the Archives give various tables of contents; to determine their sequence would be a piece of good detective work.

47   B. Lonergan, '*Insight* revisited', p. 272: 'The whole idea ['my rather theological analysis of human history'] was presented in chapter twenty of *Insight*'.

48   See note 37 above.

49   A reader for Longmans, Green & Co. is reported to have told the publishers 'You simply must publish this work. You will lose money, but you must publish it.' In fact, it turned out to be a 'best seller' within its own class, going into a second edition immediately, and reprinted over and over again. Incidentally, according to Lonergan 'The book didn't come out till '57 because Longmans Green had all their circulating capital earmarked for the next four years', *Caring*, p. 118 (on the book's sales see also ibid., pp. 219, 263).

50   Further reading (for example, Susanne Langer, Harry Stack Sullivan—he had not read them when he wrote ch. 6) led to the insertion of new footnotes. There were also revisions of the text, but there

is no evidence that this was required by the censors, who had passed
the book very expeditiously.

51 The original text and a carbon copy of these 70 pages are kept in the
Lonergan Archives.

52 Several revisions, carefully measured to replace the excised passages
and keep the pagination unchanged, were made in the second edition,
1958 (listed there, p. xv). A good number of misprints were corrected
also.

53 Mostly in the early chapters, possibly in preparation for a lecture on
the book.

54 Most notably, the Halifax lectures of 1958, now published (see note 11
above). There was an extensive set of lectures at St Mary's College,
Moraga, California, in the summer of 1961; through the enterprise of
Fr Harry Kohls we have Lonergan's own notes for these, but mostly
they are just headings. The autobiographical '*Insight* revisited' of
1973, which I have referred to so often in previous notes, is a most
reliable source—in effect, Lonergan's review-article on his own book.

55 *Understanding and Being*, pp. 72–80, 337–41, 352–5, and passim; see
the index.

56 B. Lonergan, in conversation with F. E. Crowe, July 1960.

57 See note 5 above. These three questions are not to be identified with
the triad: questions for understanding, questions for reflection, questions for deliberation. The latter three lift the subject from level to
level interiorly; the other three effect the transition from subjectivity
to objectivity (for the reflecting philosopher—unreflecting everyday
activity has no need of this transition).

58 *De intellectu et methodo*, notes of a course given at the Gregorian
University, 1959, p. 48. The notes were taken by students (F. Rossi de
Gasperis, P. J. Cahill) during the lectures.

59 For example, *Method in Theology*, p. 153 n. 1; see also '*Insight*
revisited', pp. 275–8.

60 B. Lonergan, *Philosophy of God, and Theology: The Relationship
between Philosophy of God and the Functional Specialty, Systematics*
(St Michael's Lectures, Gonzaga University, Spokane, 1972; London/
Philadelphia, 1973), pp. 11–13, 41, 64. This critique led to the erro-
neous view that Lonergan had abandoned the proof he gave in *Insight*
of the existence of God; in fact, he says in these same lectures (p. 41):
'There are proofs for the existence of God. I formulated them as best
I could in chapter nineteen of *Insight* and I'm not repudiating that at
all.'

61 See note 3 above.

62 B. Lonergan, *Verbum*, p. 53.

4

Experiments in method: a quarter-century of exploration

Bernard Lonergan taught theology for 25 years under what he called impossible conditions. Thirteen of these were in Canada (1940–53, divided evenly between the first half in Montreal and the second in Toronto), and twelve in Rome. Of Rome he later said, and the remark applies to Canada as well, 'the situation I was in was hopelessly antiquated . . . it has since been demolished'.[1]

All the same, those 25 years made a major contribution to his life-project, were indeed an indispensable condition for its completion. I do not mean that his teaching led him in a direct and steady progress toward his goal; on the contrary, it reveals various tentatives, revised and revised as the experiments continued. Nor was he altogether free to conduct his experiments in the classroom; there was a fair amount of drudgery and repetition, house-keeping chores in the theology programmes he was part of; that was a price one paid for belonging to an academic institution. But there was a difference between the basic degree courses and those he taught on the graduate level. In the former one didn't stray too far from well-trod paths—that was a price you paid for teaching seminarians, especially in Rome; on the graduate level he could test his ideas more freely, and there was probably a healthy dialectic between the two types of course. In any case, he needed those years to work out his method; there is no way to write on method in theology without direct engagement in theological questions, and that is what Lonergan's classroom duties gave him. Critics who call his method *a priori*, devised without reference to actual theology, do so surely in close to total disregard of that quarter of a century.

Method, we remember, was an early interest for Lonergan. For some time it lay fallow in his mind, but there were outcrops and it will help to collect here and amplify somewhat the points already made about this period. First of all, a negative beginning worked to his long-term advantage: he was grateful to superiors for turning him away from method in his London University programme. 'It was just as well because my own method is much better than what I would have gotten in London.'[2] But up to the summer of 1938 he did not expect to specialize in theology, so presumably any ideas he had on method would have to do with the general renovation of Catholic thought, his *Pantôn Anakephalaiôsis*. His letter of January 1935 speaks in a rather general way about the method in contemporary Catholic philosophy: 'The method is sheer make-believe but to attack a method is a grand scale operation calling for a few volumes'.[3] The decision of 1938 to send him back to Rome for doctorate studies in theology would surely have specified his search as one for theological method, but the urgency appeared on the philosophic level, in the host of disputed questions that seemed to him a scandal.[4]

Very soon therefore method began to crop up in his writings. For example, at the start of his doctoral dissertation, where he said in reference to the Banezians and Molinists, 'Unless a writer can assign a method that of itself tends to greater objectivity than those hitherto employed, his undertaking may well be regarded as superfluous'.[5] His own method will be historical and inductive, but 'there is no acceptance of the principles of positivism'; he will take a middle course which 'consists in constructing an *a priori* scheme that is capable of synthetizing any possible set of historical data . . . just as the science of mathematics constructs a generic scheme capable of synthetizing any possible set of quantitative phenomena'.[6] Such 'a general scheme of the historical process' is possible 'because the human mind is always the human mind'[7]—a maxim learned, as we saw, from Newman, and one that would direct him all his life. His introductory pages then work out this general scheme in some detail.

As the dissertation began with remarks on method, so a few years later the *verbum* articles concluded with a statement on the method employed. It 'had to be both consonant with my purpose and coherent with my conclusions'. His purpose was 'to understand what Aquinas meant by the intelligible procession of an inner word', and this meant reaching conclusions in the slow process of learning, 'the slow, repetitious, circular labor of going over and over the data'. His method united 'the ideals of the old-style manual written *ad mentem Divi Thomae* and . . . the ideal of contemporary historical study':

> Method is a means to an end; it sets forth two sets of rules—rules that facilitate collaboration and continuity of effort, and rules that guide the effort itself. The latter aim at understanding . . . method is a mere superstition when the aim of understanding is excluded. Such exclusion is the historian's temptation to positivism. On the other hand, the temptation of the manual writer is to yield to the conceptualist illusion; to think that to interpret Aquinas he has merely to quote and then argue.[8]

By this time Lonergan had come to clarity on a number of questions. One is that the focus of his work on method will very definitely be understanding:

> A method tinged with positivism would not undertake, a method affected by conceptualist illusion could not conceive, the task of developing one's own understanding so as to understand Aquinas' comprehension of understanding and of its intelligibly proceeding inner word.[9]

Another is that he has now to engage the enemy on two fronts: there is positivism, already a target in his dissertation; and there is conceptualism, which in his view fails to find the act of understanding where it really occurs; as he will say later, 'The key issue is whether concepts result from understanding or understanding results from concepts'.[10] To discover understanding where it actually occurs is to take possession of the fertile source of all concepts; to start with concepts is to cut oneself off from that fertile source.

So we come to his book on human understanding. Recall that it was intended to be 'an exploration of methods generally in preparation for a study of the method of theology', that in 1952 after three years working on the book, he learned he was to go to Rome in 1953 to teach there, so changed his plan, rounded off what he had done and published it under the title *Insight: A Study of Human Understanding*.[11] This explains what otherwise must seem curious, that the first graduate course he gave at the Gregorian University was a study of methods in general, *De methodis universim inquisitio theoretica*.[12] Why would a theologian start a new career with a course so theoretical? Why a course on method, when he has just written an enormous book on understanding? The answers are that the Gregorian University course on method was a course on the book[13] (though it was still unpublished). The book, in fact, is almost identified with methodology: 'an account of insight is an account of method';[14] and from the beginning it was conceived as a step on the way to theological method.

The fallow period has come to an end. *Insight* studied the operations that are the basis of method; work on method itself can begin in earnest now.

EXPERIMENT ONE: ANALYSIS/SYNTHESIS AS INTEGRAL STRUCTURE

All this time, and continuing through his period of teaching in Rome, Lonergan was producing for his students little supplements (*opuscula*, he called them) to the Latin textbooks used in the basic courses; moreover, students were busy taking notes on his graduate courses and multiplying them for the common good. These documents are an immense help to us as we trace Lonergan's developing thought on method; still, exemplifying his own principle that performance comes first and method later,[15] he began to introduce questions of method only about 1946. In that year he wrote a supplement on the supernatural order, *De ente supernaturali: Supplementum schematicum*,[16] and took his first step on the long road to the theological method of 1972.

His brief introduction to *De ente* . . . speaks of order in theology. Two orders are possible, one of analysis which begins from revealed truths and proceeds to their intelligible organization, and the other of synthesis which descends from that intelligible organization to the objects to be organized. Lonergan's favourite is the second, illustrated by the order in which chemistry is taught, and he justifies his choice in laconic fashion: 'Far superior is the order of synthesis (*ordo compositorius*), in which memory is not burdened and the joy of understanding banishes labor'.[17]

It remains the favourite in the programmatic article of 1954, 'Theology and understanding', where he appeals, in support of the synthetic order (*ordo disciplinae*), to Thomas's reasons for the way he wrote his *Summa Theologiae*: 'the ordinary run of books on the subject were loaded with useless questions and articles . . . they did not follow the *ordo disciplinae* . . . they kept treating the same issues over and over . . . Now in this indictment the one positive point is the *ordo disciplinae*.'[18] Of course, this agrees perfectly with Lonergan's passion for understanding and the almost daily reference in his classroom lectures to the First Vatican Council on that 'most fruitful understanding of the mysteries' which is possible to human intelligence.[19]

The long road to the theological method of 1972 would have been enormously shortened for Lonergan, could he simply have taken over Thomas's order of teaching, *ordo disciplinae*. But there exactly was the rub. Thomas could move nimbly back and forth, without much attention to the difference, between a theology using Aristotelian concepts and a Christian message that was quite un-Aristotelian, a message conceived according to other thought-patterns and delivered in quite different terms. In the twentieth century that was no longer possible; to put the problem in one word, it was history.

We shall see presently that Lonergan toward the end of his life saw his whole work as one of introducing history into theology. That is certainly a problem in his analysis/synthesis stage in the 1950s, but perhaps he had not yet seen it in its full dimensions, for the 1954 article discusses it in a kind of appendix, and in his full-scale study of analysis/synthesis in 1957, he tries to attach history to that pair as a subsequent factor. The fit is awkward. So is the way he at this time conceives the analytic side of the pair: a little too simply as analysis, without full recognition of the role of history as a factor prior to analysis. What is at first a liberating idea can become a straitjacket.

It was analysis and history, and their relation, that would give him trouble for years. Positive theology had made its entry at least four centuries earlier, it had become a standard part of theological courses, but lacking the guiding hand of Thomas Aquinas here, theologians made various attempts to deal with it. The textbooks in Lonergan's time tended to mingle in disorder elements that he would distinguish and assign to separate analytic and synthetic branches.

In any case, if we expect his love for Thomas and synthetic understanding to lead him to shortchange somewhat the positive part of theology, we will be badly mistaken: he knew from the start that the synthesis which gives systematic understanding needs the mediating basis and complement of the analytic order, the order of discovery, which proceeds from what is given in Scripture, the first for us, the *priora quoad nos*, to what is most fundamental, the first in itself, the *prius quoad se*.

Thus in trinitarian theology, the order of analysis is from the missions of Son and Spirit in the New Testament, first to their consubstantiality with the Father, then to the distinction of the Three by mutually opposed relations, and finally to the processions understood through the psychological analogy. This path is roughly the path of actual history, from New Testament through Nicaea and the Cappadocians to Augustine. The synthetic order of Thomas Aquinas moves in exactly the opposite direction, beginning with the processions, moving to the relations, then to the persons, and so to the missions of Son and Spirit.

Here in that synthetic order, with its model in Aquinas and its goal in systematic understanding, Lonergan was perfectly at home. It remained an important factor in his definitive theological method some years later;[20] indeed, for most of the 1940s and 1950s, it was more than an important factor: it was almost theology *tout court*. Thus in the little work of 1956 on the psychology and ontology of Christ, with its odd title *De constitutione Christi ontologica et psychologica supplementum confecit Bernardus Lonergan, S.I.*, he comes in the third part to the question of theological understanding. Positive theology receives a token mention, but his interest is in speculative theology and its method. There is an analogy between metaphysical science and theological science, which he sets forth, without a word of explanation for the title, as *De Methodorum Analogia*;[21] 'science' and 'method' seem almost interchangeable, and science means synthetic understanding.

ENTER HISTORY: NEW WINE, OLD BOTTLES

I have said that the analytic order gave Lonergan enormous trouble. Since it was, in fact, the actual historical order of discovery, it brought with it all the complexity of history, and how to understand history was a question he would wrestle with in nearly every work he wrote at this time.[22] Only when he came to terms with that question could he get analysis into perspective and provide a basis for the systematic understanding that was his first love.

The first major work to take up this complex of questions, raised already in the 1954 article and curiously downplayed in the 1956 booklet on Christology, is the very thorough work of 1957, so oddly titled again that we have to give the Latin in full: *Divinarum personarum conceptionem analogicam evolvit Bernardus Lonergan S.I.*—Bernard Lonergan's own analogical concept of the divine persons! The long introductory chapter to that work is a full-scale treatise on method in theology. The goal is theological understanding, but the theologian moves toward that goal in three distinct ways, and in these three ways we have Lonergan's first great effort to get the whole approach to theology into a single integral and coherent framework.[23]

There is analysis, which may be named also the way of reduction to causes, resolution and analysis having the same meaning in their respective Latin and Greek roots; or the way of discovery, since previously unknown causes are uncovered in this way; or the way of certitude, as beginning with and basing itself on what is most manifest. There is synthesis, which may be named also the way of composition, bringing causes together to constitute things; or the way of doctrine or teaching, beginning from the most fundamental concepts to achieve understanding of the whole science.

These two ways of proceeding he illustrates, as he so often did, by the difference between the history of an empirical science and the manual used to teach the science itself to students. Historically every science starts from what is observed, but manuals used for teaching the science do not start there; they start with the idea most fundamental to the science. Lonergan's examples start with his favourite, used in the 1954 article, in the 1956 Christology, and occurring over and over again, namely the periodic table in chemistry; but he adds others now: Newton's laws of motion, Riemannian geometry, and the operators of quanta.[24]

It is the third movement that captures our interest. Analysis leads to synthesis, but analysis itself moves forward, correcting earlier analysis, and in its next stage leads to another synthesis which may be a total revision of the former one. The ongoing sequence of this alternation is the history of the science.[25] It seems, then, that at this time the historical movement is put in the context of, and is quite subordinate to, the first two movements. That is true of the organization not only of this chapter in Lonergan, but also of the whole treatise where throughout twelve years he most assiduously applied his method: the doctrine of the Trinity.

The structure of analysis/synthesis had, then, a strong grip on Lonergan's thinking, and through several years maintained its hold on him. Nevertheless, at the end of the day it would be the historical that would dominate, and this triumph was already programmed, as hindsight now enables us to see, in the two long sections of the present work that he devotes to the movement of history.[26]

The question is treated in roughly the following order. First, there are the historical differences we may name cultural; they raise a serious problem for a Church that began in a particular culture but is by definition universal, namely, the problem of finding a transcultural principle. For Christians this was illustrated at the very beginning in the dispute over application of the Mosaic law to Gentile believers.

How are we to handle the problem? There is some help in the spontaneous symbols studied in depth psychology, for they have a transcultural force; again, the efforts of scholars to enter into the culture and mentality of another time aim at the same goal in another way. Ultimately, however, these and all other means prove inadequate unless we appeal to truths which interiorly we find to be absolute.[27]

Lonergan maintains that the problem forces us to enlarge our notions of the 'first for us'. The 'first in itself' may be stable; not so the 'first for us', which changes with the times, and so is not the same in scriptural times, patristic times, and the various other times of history. Further, we must distinguish transcultural process, theological process, and dogmatic process. The transcultural process moves from the scriptural 'first for us' to the patristic 'first for us', and on to the particular 'first for us' of any other culture. The theological process moves from the 'first for us' (scriptural and patristic especially) to the 'first in itself', to what is systematically prior. The dogmatic process is that whereby the systematic 'first' is supported by the *magisterium* of the Church.

All this sounds terribly abstract. Lonergan, however, does not leave it there; he illustrates it in four examples of actual historical process. True, the history is related in somewhat schematic fashion, so it may help the present reader if we fill in the scheme a little. What, then, is the 'first for us' in the New Testament view of Jesus? It is seen in some one or other (or combination thereof) of the 46 names that I believe have been found for him there; thus, he is son of David, or the great prophet, or the apocalyptic son of man, or the Messiah, or the son of God, or the word of God—any or all of these would convey an immediate meaning to the people of Palestine. But none of them alone was found sufficient by the 318 bishops at the First Council of Nicaea to state what the Word was fundamentally, what the 'first in itself' was that would give a basis to their faith in him, and so to all the 46 names. For this the Council had to create, or borrow, another language: God from God, Light from Light, true God from true God, begotten not made, consubstantial with the Father.

With that brief illustration we may make more sense out of Lonergan's first example of actual historical process—that of Nicaea in 325, when the scriptural 'first' gave way to 'consubstantial', the *homoousion*—and form at least a notional apprehension of the other three: that of Chalcedon in 451, when the patristic first (their view of 'nature' as a complete concrete being) gave way to the doctrine of two natures in Christ; that of the Middle Ages when theology moved to the systematic first; that of later centuries (our own), when the mounting uncertainties that result from the previous three examples initiated the methodological movement.[28]

As far as I know, this was Lonergan's first sustained excursus into the relation of history to theology. It was a major effort, but still in the nature of an excursus; he returned in the next section to the real focus, the object of theology, a field far more familiar to scholastic thought. That return is a sign, I would say, of the continuing dominance in his thinking of the object of theology. We saw that dominance maintained in the 1954 article 'Theology and understanding', and we see it maintained too in a letter, written about the same time as the article, where he gives a progress report on his thinking at the time:

> The Method of Theology is coming into perspective. For the Trinity: Imago Dei in homine and proceed to the limit . . . For the rest: ordo universi. From the viewpoint of theology, it is a manifold of unities developing in relation to one another and in relation to God . . . From the viewpoint of religious experience, it is the same relations as lived in a development from elementary intersubjectivity . . . to intersubjectivity in Christ (cf. the endless Pauline . . . sun- compounds) on the sensitive (external Church, sacraments, sacrifice, liturgy) and intellectual levels (faith, hope, charity). Religious Experience : Theology : Dogma : : Potency : Form : Act.[29]

A schematic report indeed! Nevertheless that letter, in its parallel statements on religious experience and theology, suggests the emergence of a new direction. The 1954 article hints at the same revolution in thought; though it dealt mostly with theology as science in the Aristotelian sense—Lonergan was conservative on that during this middle period of his development—it ended with indications of a quite different orientation, a section on 'Contemporary methodological issues', as the 1988 editors named it from a phrase in its opening paragraph, or a kind of appendix, as I referred to it earlier.

In that 'appendix' Lonergan lists four issues that are not wholly amenable to previous notions of science.[30] There are, first, the patterns of human experience—roughly, the differentiations of consciousness of his later thinking—and so the problem of transposing from one to the other. Next, 'there is the problem of the relations between speculative and positive theology'. A 'flood tide of scholarly diligence' has yielded 'a vast multiplicity'. Lonergan refuses to believe 'that scientific method in the historical sciences is free from higher-level controls and permanently dedicated to the exclusive production of unrelated monographs'. But how are we to reduce the 'vast multiplicity' to anything like a manageable unity? 'Thirdly, there is the problem of the relations between speculative theology and the empirical human sciences.' The latter have only recently appeared on the scene; they are not subject to the philosophy through which theology once exercised her control over empirical science, for they deal with the human race in the concrete —suffering the effects of sin, in need of grace, and so demanding a direct relation to theology. There is, finally, the historical problem of the role understanding played in the work of Thomas Aquinas—a problem that is more than historical, for it impinges on our own need to overcome conceptualism, and thus on problems of theological method.

The documents of the mid-1950s reveal, therefore, an inner tension in Lonergan's thinking. Changing ideas of theology are changing his idea of theological method. To adapt a phrase he used in regard to Thomas, the new wine of historical studies is bursting the old bottles of Aristotelian terminology. The object has been dominant, but the subject, the believing and thinking theologian, is assuming greater and greater importance. The unity of theology is still achieved on a conceptual basis, but the way is opening to the unity of the eight functional specialties of *Method in Theology*. Thus, we agree completely with a remark he made as he concluded his 1957 exposition, that a complete methodological treatise would require a more ample and profound development.[31] Yes, indeed, and require it not just in the objective exposition of his method, but more radically still in himself, the theologian and methodologist.

His successive efforts to achieve that development have now to be sketched.

I believe there was a significant step forward, at least in his grasp of historicity, of the gap between the origins of our faith and the statements of theology, in the course of lectures he gave in the spring semester of 1959 at the Gregorian University: *De intellectu et methodo*.[32] Eight years before, he had lectured on 'Intelligence and reality'; now the English of his title would be 'Intelligence and method'—a revealing change.[33] The next year he would give a course on 'System and history', *De systemate et historia*, also a revealing title, for it shows in the starkest way the two poles of the tension in his thinking, but that course is less well documented. The 1959 course, in contrast, was carefully reported;[34] we will therefore take that year as benchmark for this stage of Lonergan's development.

There is another reason for doing so. We have also for that year a source in English, and it is directly from Lonergan. A paper in the Archives entitled 'Method in Catholic theology' is for whole passages simply the English of *De intellectu et methodo*, giving us an authoritative check on the Latin notes. The occasion of the paper is not indicated, but it is almost certainly the lecture given to the Society for the Study of Theology in Nottingham, 15 April 1959.[35] We shall return presently to this document.

The problem Lonergan has been wrestling with, and tackles again with a new approach in his 1959 Latin course, is that of history and system. In Catholic theology this takes the concrete form of the difference between the sources of theology and theology itself, and of the way you move from one to the other. He sees three aspects to the problem: foundations, historicity, alienation ('De triplici problemate: fundamenti–historicitatis–chasmatis').[36] The first is the problem of transition from one ordering of doctrine or theology to another, the second is the problem of continuity throughout the orderings, and the third is the problem of the ever greater systematizing of an ordering, for that takes us further and further from our sources.[37] Lonergan struggles with this triple problem through fifteen legal-size pages of single-spaced Latin.[38]

First the problem of foundations, which in this work is not a problem of what is given in revelation, but one of transition from that firm base to another expression. There is a leap from the scriptures to theology, from Paul to Thomas Aquinas. We do not, he says, justify the leap by the external form of words we use (one may think here of the fundamentalists, for whom words are foundational); nor through manipulation of concepts and judgements alone (one may think here of the conceptualists) for that works only within a system—deduction is helpless when questions arise that the system cannot account for. Lonergan's own solution builds on his previous work. It is to go behind the words, behind the concepts and judgements, in his habitual appeal to intelligence itself and its three-fold formation through understanding, science, and wisdom. This is familiar ground to his readers, though there is something new in the searching dialectic to which he submits the notion of wisdom.

The problems of historicity and alienation are dealt with more briefly (the three problems, he has said, are really one), by invoking the twofold order of analysis and synthesis, the duality of human consciousness (we may think here of the common sense and theory of *Insight*) with the resulting divergence in thought-patterns, or the development of understanding which gives different historical conceptions of the same reality.

The second part of the course deals more directly with method; this is the part Lonergan took up in the Nottingham lecture, so we can turn now from his Latin course to his English lecture. He formulates five rules: 'Understand. Understand systematically. Reverse counter-positions. Develop positions. Accept the responsibility of judgment.'[39] We recognize here the influence of *Insight*, but Lonergan relates the rules to history in a new way. 'The rules seem to be immanent in history', he says, illustrating the first from the twelfth century, the second from the thirteenth, the third from the fourteenth, and the fourth from 'a subsequent and still expanding inquiry'.[40]

The rules are not just immanent in factual history; they are relevant to the very notion of historical theology. This is a new area unknown to mediaeval theology:

> The achievement of the thirteenth century is not a goal but a starting-point. In particular, it lacked what we call the historical sense, namely, an awareness that concepts are functions of time, that they change and develop with every advance of understanding, that they become platitudinous and insignificant by passing through minds that do not understand, and that such changes take place in a determinate manner that can be the object of a science.[41]

Lonergan believes that his general rules have a role in uniting speculative and historical theology, the thirteenth and the nineteenth centuries, that simply because they are general they are no less applicable to historical than to speculative theology. He continues as follows:

> . . . because they are rules, because they are dynamic, they serve to unite historical and speculative theology as past process and present term. Historical or positive theology is concerned with the becoming of speculative; and speculative theology is the term of historical process. To add positive to speculative theology is not to add something quite extrinsic; it is not to add a new and autonomous department that goes its own independent way. Rather, I should say, historical theology is speculative theology becoming conscious of its origins and its development and, at the same time, speculative theology is just the contemporary stage of the movement that historical theology examines and analyses. To overlook or to reject that unity has, I believe, only one result. On the one hand, historical theology becomes lost in the wilderness of universal history; it ceases to be a distinct discipline with a proper field and competence of its own; for it is only from speculative theology that historical can learn just what its precise field is and what are the inner laws of that field in their enduring manifestations. On the other hand, speculative theology withers away; for its proper task is, not just understanding, but understanding the faith; its positive basis is historical and without that basis it may retire into an ivory tower to feed itself with subtle memories, it may merge with the general stream of philosophic thought, or it may attempt to take over, modestly or despotically, the teaching office of the Church, but the one thing necessary it cannot do, continue today the process begun so long ago of adding to living faith the dimension of systematic understanding.[42]

Lonergan's fifth rule returns to his traditional view on revelation and truth, with interesting additions, but not yet with the perspective he will achieve a few years later:

> In other fields, understanding begins not from truths but from data. It is understanding that will promote data to the level of truth, and the truth to be attained is no guiding presence but an ideal whose precise features are not to be discerned. In theology, things are otherwise. There are, indeed, data that are just data as in the other sciences: most exegetical and historical questions are

of that character. But there are also truths, and understanding them involves a reversal of roles; where in other fields understanding precedes and determines truth, in theology understanding follows and is determined.

Now this reversal of roles gives rise to special techniques that centre about the true proposition, the logic of presuppositions and implications, and the semantics or metaphysics of meaning. My one observation is that they are techniques; they serve to chart the path of efforts to understand; but they are not ends; they provide the scaffolding needed to build the theological edifice; but they are not the edifice itself, the understanding sought by faith; they serve to delimit and to define what is to be understood, but the understanding is something more. It lies in the realm of analogy and in the intelligible interlocking of the truths of faith.[43]

Here we see theology tied and restricted to its older formulation, *fides quaerens intellectum*. It begins from revealed truths; its business is to understand them. With present hindsight, we can say that this represents the sixth and seventh functional specialties, doctrines and systematics. There are in the general area of religious studies data that are just data, but that field seems to lie outside theology proper. Lonergan has not yet reached the point where he can see theology itself starting with data, unfolding in the three functions of research, interpretation, and history, and finding a hinge in dialectic and foundations to turn from these mediating functions to the traditional mediated theology. He is on the way to his empirical view of theology, where data can be treated as data, in study that is an intrinsic part of theology, not a mere auxiliary discipline, but at present the honourable name of theology is still restricted to the old *fides quaerens intellectum*.

FROM HISTORY TO METHOD

Lonergan continued to work out his ideas in the arena of his annual graduate courses, and so in 1961–62 we have a new course with a new title and a decisive further step toward the definitive approach of *Method in Theology* ten years later. This course is called *De methodo theologiae* in its Latin form at the Gregorian University, or 'The method of theology' in English lectures given immediately afterwards in the summer of 1962, at Regis College, Toronto. Both the Latin notes and the transcription of the English tape-recordings are available for study;[44] we will follow the latter.

Again, I find the title itself to be significant in the evolution of Lonergan's theological method: method had been a kind of corollary to the philosophic study of human understanding, or part of the prolegomena to a methodical theology; now it is neither corollary nor prolegomenon but the focal topic. The content corresponds: the first day the lectures speak of the *method* in express contrast to the *object* of theology; method is specified in terms of operations, the operations are those of a subject, and the subject is discussed under the headings of horizon, conversion, authenticity, and so on. The 'turn to the subject'—a phrase many use to describe the character of these years—is well established. Of course, there is continuity: the object too is to be studied, but through the operations of the subject; that is the methodical viewpoint. Equally significant is the direction taken on the second day of lectures, when the discussion turns first to values and the good, and then to meaning, for human development is constituted by meaning. Readers of the 1972 *Method* will recognize this sequence: it anticipates the first three chapters of that book.[45]

We may conclude this section with a word on Lonergan's *De Deo Trino* of 1964.[46] It is his swan-song in traditional scholastic theology —or maybe we should say 'school' or 'seminary' theology, for Lonergan was always scholastic with a difference—but also it incorporates a number of the ideas we have just been discussing, and thus presents a curious combination of old and new. One suspects a compromise with the 'realities' of a teaching institution. Textbooks were a necessity; the two volumes of previous editions of Lonergan's trinitarian textbook added up to 628 pages; he was not about to undertake the Herculean labour of a complete revision, especially when it appeared that he would now be relieved of this teaching chore; so he made such revisions as he could conveniently manage, and issued the book in its third and final form.

Naturally the Introduction to the first part is the best index to his present orientation, and it is there in fact that major revisions are made. He calls the Introduction 'Dogmatic development', and we notice that the whole first part has become 'Dogmatic Part' instead of 'Analytic Part'—a change I take to mean that history is not just history. What he said in 1959 still holds: in history we have a transcultural process, a theological process, and a dogmatic process.

There are four aspects to this dogmatic development. In the

objective aspect there is the difference in literary genre between the gospels and dogma. In the subjective aspect the objective is traced back to the difference between differentiated and undifferentiated consciousness. The third aspect is evaluative—a matter of defending dogma against its critics; this of course is a familiar story in Lonergan: he has been defending the value of dogmas through all his theological work.[47] Fourthly, there is the hermeneutical aspect. The basic need, as we might expect, is for a sound philosophy:

If one has a false cognitional theory, a false epistemology, or a false metaphysics, one will have little or no understanding of defined dogmas (not without reason are philosophical studies placed before the study of theology); but the same errors and the same tendencies, more or less, which now render dogmas unintelligible or unacceptable, were at work implicitly before the dogmas emerged in the first place, exerting a covert influence against their emergence.[48]

1965: BREAKTHROUGH WITHOUT ENCIRCLEMENT

In *Insight* Lonergan used a military metaphor of breakthrough, encirclement, and confinement to describe the evidence for a metaphysics.[49] It has been studied far too little, in my opinion, with resulting misunderstandings in many areas and especially in regard to the famous chapter 19 of the book. That, however, is not the present point. I recall the metaphor here because the first two stages seem to describe also the present advances: that of 1965 and that of the years that intervened before *Method in Theology* was published in 1972; there was a breakthrough to the eight functional specialties in February of 1965, but there was not yet the encirclement that only a whole new set of categories would make possible; those needed categories were not yet fully elaborated.

The structures of cognitional process and reality, and their isomorphism, were the special contributions of the 1940s and 1950s to Lonergan's integral view; the 1965 breakthrough was itself very largely a matter of enlarging the structure and setting it up in relation to the eight functions of theology—for example, there is clear emergence now of the fourth level to give the integral structure. But the categories had to be worked out (or, as was often the case, borrowed and reworked) that would be appropriate for the turn to the subject, and this turn, begun in the Existentialism lectures of

1957, became a preoccupation of his in the 1960s: meaning, value, mediation, authenticity, dialectic, conversion, differentiations of consciousness, and so on.[50] This work continued for some years after the 1965 breakthrough; if that breakthrough belongs rather to our next chapter, the work of the 1960s in establishing categories belongs rather to this one.

The whole decade of the 1960s was, in fact, a very creative period, as creative for *Method in Theology* as 1949–53 had been for *Insight*, though the creativity shows up in a different way; that is, whereas *Insight* plunged into our world like a meteor, almost without warning, we see the elements of *Method* being assembled almost before our eyes in a way that seems piecemeal. Thus, we have a series of lectures in which Lonergan works out these categories: a lecture on the philosophy of history in 1960;[51] a triad on meaning: 'Time and meaning' in 1962,[52] 'The analogy of meaning' in 1963,[53] and 'Dimensions of meaning' in 1965;[54] lectures also on the theology of history (1963),[55] on the transition to historical mindedness (1966),[56] on the new context of theology (1967),[57] and an explosion of lectures in 1968, including a key exposition of the subject symbolizing the new turn.[58]

There is no retrievable parallel, in the preparation of *Insight*, to this piecemeal assembly of elements. Even in the sets of lectures that attempted an integral view of elements assembled to date, the preparation for *Method* was more abundant.[59] These sets need a study in detail that cannot be undertaken here. Besides the more integral view they afford, we see a full exposition of the particular elements as these one by one enter the picture. Thus, hermeneutics was the topic of a lecture in the Regis College Institute on Method in 1962; a widely circulated copy gave a preview of chapter 7 of the book that would appear only ten years later.[60] In the same Institute we have the emergence of antithetical worlds: the sacred and the profane, the external and the internal, the world of common sense and the world of theory. The worlds do not easily interpenetrate one another; hence the integrated person is one who can move readily from one to the other, and to handle this passage from world to world Lonergan develops from Hegel and others the notion of mediation.[61] This latter concept was very thoroughly worked out the following year in the Gonzaga University lectures of 1963,[62] and found religious application in a lecture on 'The mediation of Christ in prayer'.[63] There seem to have been important developments in the Georgetown University lectures of 1964. Though these are not well documented,[64] the notes available show gaps being filled. Thus, we now have three approaches to data: there are data that are just data, in the natural sciences; data with meaning, in the human sciences; and data with a meaning that is true, in theological science.[65] Again, foundations is emerging as a function distinct from the fundamental theology of the past,[66] and in anticipation of the 1968 lecture, there is a discussion of the normative subject, the truncated subject, the actual subject, and the existential subject.[67]

That 1968 lecture, called simply 'The subject', is a milestone in the steady turn to the subject already mentioned. For the divisions of the Georgetown University lectures it substitutes The Neglected Subject, The Truncated Subject, The Immanentist Subject, The Existential Subject, and The Alienated Subject. Then under the heading of The Existential Subject, Lonergan develops his new notion of value.[68] Whereas in *Insight* the good was the intelligible and reasonable (this was Lonergan's rather intellectualist period), it now becomes an intentional response to feeling in values. It belongs to a fourth level of consciousness that is clearly distinct from and clearly goes beyond the three cognitional levels. Where earlier Lonergan's model might have been the mind of Thomas, restless till it could rest in seeing God, now he leans more to the heart of Augustine, restless till it rests in God. And so his favourite text from Scripture becomes Romans 5:5, on God's love flooding our hearts through the Holy Spirit who is given to us.[69]

Besides the new notion of value, two categories which preoccupy Lonergan during these years are meaning and history.

In the first half of the 1960s meaning becomes fully domiciled in the Lonergan house of ideas. It is not just meaning as pertaining to cognitional operations—that had been a factor in *Insight* and before that in the *verbum* articles—but meaning now as constitutive of human institutions. A favourite example is the lawcourt: 'Lawcourts without meaning are sound and fury'.[70] Again, what is revelation? It is a new meaning added to human life. What is the body of Christ? It is a new order; just as the family, the state, the economy, the law express an order with a meaning constitutive of the human good, so also the body of Christ is an order, a redemptive order that counteracts the evil of sin in the social mediation of the human good.[71]

Not only is human activity constituted formally by the intentional, by meaning, but this develops, it is historical. The work of Leopold von Ranke (1795–1886) and Wilhelm Dilthey (1833–1911) has enormous importance in the problem of contemporary theology; historical studies penetrate or inundate theology. If we get the import of this movement we will know what has been disturbing theology over the past fifty years.[72]

We therefore come back again to history. For the effort of the 1950s to attach history in some way to analysis/synthesis had proved inadequate, and Lonergan continued to work on the problem. Late in life, in fact, he would say 'All my work has been introducing history into Catholic theology'.[73] It was his whole work because it was the problem of our times: 'The whole problem in modern theology, Protestant and Catholic, is the introduction of historical scholarship'.[74] These very forthright statements during interviews are not mere accidents of conversation; a published paper of 1968 says

> Since the beginning of the century theologians have been incorporating more and more historical study into their theology . . . But mere history is not theology, and the task of doing genuine history and on that basis proceeding to theology confronts Catholic theologians with the most basic and far-reaching of problems, the problem of method in theology.[75]

Even in old age he was still hopeful about the contribution of the Second Vatican Council to this problem: 'The meaning of Vatican II was the acknowledgement of history'.[76]

The reader will, of course, remember that 30 years earlier history had already been an important category for Lonergan, and will wonder why I make such a big deal of it in his development during the 1960s. The difference is that there is the history that happens and there is the history that is written about the events that happen. One has been with us since the human race began, the other has a more recent pedigree, and in fact became a theological problem only in the last two centuries, and became a problem for Lonergan only when he tried to assimilate those two centuries. It is the question of historical scholarship, quite different from the analysis of history he attempted in the 1930s.

True, he had the two meanings of history and their distinction clear in the papers of the 1930s, but it was the first, the history that happens, that captured his interest then, not only in its theological structure of progress, decline, and redemption (I use his later terms) but even in its concrete and temporal sequences. He acknowledges the history that is written, but he does not see it as a problem. He had not yet assimilated the work of the German Historical School to which he will so often refer in his later years. Human historicity in the sense of cultural differences between times, between peoples of the same time, had not entered deeply into his thinking, though he credits his reading of Christopher Dawson in the 1930s with starting him in that direction.[77] It seems, in fact, that it was his reluctant move to Rome in 1953, and the resulting closer contact with European currents of thought, that opened up for him this area;[78] if that is the case, we can never be sufficiently grateful to the religious superiors who transferred him to Rome, much though it seemed at the time to interfere with his plans.

It has been a long road, an uphill climb, with a succession of plateaus reached along the way, each with its fascinating views. But there remains the pass through the mountains and the world to be revealed and explored on the other side. Lonergan was not to explore that new country in any detail at all, but he did, I believe, discover the pass to take us through what he once called the 'impenetrable wall' that scholarship (read: the German Historical School) had set up between theology and its sources.[79] Metaphors, however, become boring if carried too far. It will be the business of our next chapter to describe in its own proper terms the way Lonergan implemented his 1965 breakthrough.

Notes

1 B. Lonergan, 'An interview with Fr. Bernard Lonergan, S.J.' in *A Second Collection*, ed. W. Ryan and B. Tyrrell (London/Philadelphia, 1974/1975), p. 212 (see Chapter 1, note 51 above). There is perhaps a measure of hindsight in these denunciations: when theology was simply systematic, one person could teach it reasonably well; it was when data became the starting point, and research, interpretation and history became intrinsic functions of theology, that the conditions became impossible; but that was a later development in Lonergan.

2 P. Lambert, C. Tansey and C. Going (eds), *Caring about Meaning: Patterns in the Life of Bernard Lonergan* (Montreal, 1982), p. 10.

3 B. Lonergan, letter to Henry Keane, 22 January 1935, p. 8.

4 See Chapter 3, note 10 above.

5 B. Lonergan, 'The *Gratia Operans* dissertation: Preface and Introduction', *Method: Journal of Lonergan Studies* 3/2 (October 1985), p. 10; this was not published with the articles of 1941–42, or with the book of 1971.

6 Ibid., p. 11.

7 Ibid., p. 12. See Chapter 1, note 40 above.

8 B. Lonergan, *Verbum: Word and Idea in Aquinas*, ed. D. Burrell (Notre Dame/London, 1967/1968), pp. 215–16.

9 Ibid., p. 217.

10 B. Lonergan, *Method in Theology* (London, 1972), p. 336 n. 1.

11 See Chapter 3, note 9 above.

12 *Liber Annualis* (Rome, 1955), p. 338.

13   B. Lonergan, letter to F. E. Crowe, 24 September 1954: 'I am giving a
      course on Insight . . . De methodis universim . . .'.

14   B. Lonergan, *Insight: A Study of Human Understanding* (2nd edn;
      London/New York, 1958), p. 270.

15   B. Lonergan, 'Method: trend and variations' in *A Third Collection*,
      ed. F. E. Crowe (New York/London, 1985), p. 13: 'normally scien-
      tific development is a jump ahead of scientific method. Performance
      comes first. Once performance occurs, especially when successful per-
      formance occurs, there follows reflection. Only as a series of diverse
      reflections are pieced together, do there begin to emerge and take
      shape the prescriptions of a scientific method.'

16   It was a set of notes for a course on divine grace that he gave at the
      Collège de l'Immaculée-Conception, Montreal, in the fall of 1946.
      They have been reissued at various times and in various places, but the
      critical text, which remains unpublished, was prepared by F. E.
      Crowe, C. O'Donovan and G. Sala, Regis College, Toronto, 1973.

17   B. Lonergan, *De ente supernaturali*, p. 2 (see the preceding note).

18   B. Lonergan, 'Theology and understanding', in *Collection*, ed. F. E.
      Crowe and R. M. Doran (2nd edn; *Collected Works of Bernard
      Lonergan* 4; Toronto, 1988), p. 121.

19   *Constitutio dogmatica 'Dei Filius' de fide catholica*, cap. 4 ('De fide et
      ratione'). In the Denzinger–Bannwart edition of the *Enchiridion Sym-
      bolorum*, which Lonergan used most of his life, the marginal number
      for this passage (1796) became firmly lodged in the memory of his
      students.

20   B. Lonergan, *Method in Theology*, pp. 345–6. See also his
      'Christology today: methodological reflections' in *A Third Collec-
      tion*, p. 96 n. 10: 'Aquinas composed his *Summa Theologiae* in the *via
      doctrinae*. . . . It corresponds to the functional specialty, *Systematics*,
      of my *Method in Theology*. The *via inventionis* would cover the first
      four or perhaps five previous specialties.'

21   B. Lonergan, *De constitutione Christi ontologica et psychologica*
      (Rome, 1956), pp. 44–9. Though he had worked out the analytic/
      synthetic approach in 'Theology and understanding' two years before
      (see note 18 above), Lonergan did not apply it in this work of
      Christology. Why? True, the main interest of this booklet is in the
      ontology and psychology of Christ, but it is curious that nowhere in
      his Christology did Lonergan take up the question of method the way
      he did in his trinitarian theology. I suspect that he did not find here the
      guidance from Thomas Aquinas that he found on the Trinity.

22   Besides his lectures and writings, there is his testimony in interviews;
      see *Caring*, p. 59: between *Insight* and *Method* 'I had to master inter-
      pretation and history and dialectic and get them in perspective'; p. 26:
      'I had to go into history and interpretation, and into *Verstehen*'.

23   *Divinarum personarum conceptionem analogicam evolvit Bernardus
      Lonergan S. I.* (Rome, 1957), cap. 1, sectio 4a: De triplici motu quo ad
      finem procedatur (pp. 20–3).

24   Ibid. See also the long comparison of the first two ways that follows in
      section 5, Comparantur motus analyticus et syntheticus (pp. 23–8);
      analysis and synthesis are still up front in Lonergan's search for

method, but it is indicative that so much space is given to the question of history (see note 26 below).

25 Ibid., Sectio 4a, p. 21.

26 Ibid., Sectio 6a: Tertii et historici motus additur consideratio (pp. 28–34); Sectio 7a: Motus historici consideratio ulterior (pp. 34–41).

27 Ibid., in Sectio 6a, pp. 29–31.

28 Ibid., Sectio 7a, pp. 35–9.

29 B. Lonergan, letter to F.E. Crowe, 5 May 1954 (I have made slight corrections to Lonergan's typing).

30 B. Lonergan, 'Theology and understanding' in *Collection*, pp. 127–32.

31 B. Lonergan, *Divinarum personarum*, p. 48.

32 *De intellectu et methodo*, notes of a course given at the Gregorian University, 1959; see Chapter 3, note 58 above.

33 The sequence in the titles of the three sets of lectures is interesting: 'Thought and reality' (1945–46), 'Intelligence and reality' (1951), 'Intelligence and method' (1959).

34 F. Rossi de Gasperis (co-reporter with P. J. Cahill) checked the *reportatio* with Lonergan (this information I have from Matthew Lamb). The Lonergan Archives has notes taken by Rossi de Gasperis the following year on the course *De systemate et historia*, not yet transferred to type; also notes with the same title among Lonergan's papers, no doubt pertaining to this course.

35 'Method in Catholic theology', reported in the 'Chronica' of the university's *Liber Annualis* (1960), p. 109.

36 B. Lonergan, *De intellectu et methodo*, p. 11.

37 Compare B. Lonergan, *Method in Theology*, p. 276: 'Scholarship builds an impenetrable wall between systematic theology and its historical religious sources'.

38 *De intellectu et methodo*, pp. 11–25.

39 'Method in Catholic theology', p. 2 of typescript.

40 Ibid., p. 23.

41 Ibid.

42 Ibid., pp. 29–30.

43 Ibid., p. 30.

44 The Latin notes, *De methodo theologiae*, have 60 legal-size pages with the notation 'Notae desumptae ab alumnis—1962'; the notation could mislead us, for the notes, as far as they go, correspond exactly to Lonergan's own lecture notes and were surely copied from them (Lonergan Archives, Batch V, File 1—dated, showing the last lecture as given on 28 May 1962). The lectures in the Institute on 'The method of theology', Regis College, Toronto, 9–20 July 1962, change the order of topics followed in the notes and go considerably further; tape-recordings and various transcriptions of the Institute lectures are available at the Lonergan Research Institute.

45 B. Lonergan, *Method in Theology*; chs 1–3 are on, respectively, Method, The Human Good, and Meaning.

46 B. Lonergan, *De Deo Trino*, 2 vols (Rome, 1964). Vol. I (Pars Dogmatica) is a second edition of *De Deo Trino: Pars analytica*

(Rome, 1961); the first part of this first volume has been translated by C. O'Donovan, *The Way to Nicea: The Dialectical Development of Trinitarian Theology* (London/Philadelphia, 1976). Vol. II (Pars Synthetica) is the third edition of *Divinarum personarum*.

47   He continues to defend their value against E. Voegelin, though in relatively mild terms, 'Theology and praxis' in *A Third Collection*, p. 195.

48   *The Way to Nicea*, p. 8.

49   *Insight: A Study of Human Understanding*, pp. 484, 521-2, 570-1; the 'envelopment' of p. 484 is changed to 'encirclement' in the next two references.

50   I remember a conversation when he passed through Toronto on his way to Gonzaga University, Spokane, in the summer of 1963, in which he remarked that he was carrying 'three shopping bags'—one held notes on mediation, another notes on meaning, but I have forgotten what the contents of the third were.

51   B. Lonergan, 'Notes from the introductory lecture in the philosophy of history', unpublished lecture at Thomas More Institute, Montreal, 23 September 1960.

52   B. Lonergan, 'Time and meaning', *Bernard Lonergan: Three Lectures* (Montreal, 1975), 2nd lecture, pp. 29-54. The lecture was given 25 September 1962.

53   B. Lonergan, 'The analogy of meaning', unpublished lecture at Thomas More Institute, Montreal, 24 September 1963.

54   B. Lonergan, 'Dimensions of meaning', ch. 16 in *Collection*, pp. 232-45; the lecture was given at Marquette University, Milwaukee, 12 May 1965.

55   B. Lonergan, 'De theologia historiae', unpublished lecture at the Capranica College, Rome, 27 March 1963.

56   B. Lonergan, 'The transition from a classicist world-view to historical-mindedness' in *A Second Collection*, pp. 1-9, a lecture at Regis College, Toronto, 10 September 1966, and at a seminar of the Canon Law Society of America, in October of that year.

57   B. Lonergan, 'Theology in its new context' in *A Second Collection*, pp. 55-67, a lecture at the 'Congress on the theology of the renewal of the Church, centenary of Canada, 1867-1967', Toronto, July 1967, under the title, 'The new context of theology'.

58   B. Lonergan, 'The subject' in *A Second Collection*, pp. 69-86, also published separately as *The Aquinas Lecture* (Marquette University, Milwaukee, 3 March 1968).

59   For lectures on the way to *Insight*, see Chapter 3 above. More or less integral sets of lectures on the way to *Method* were given at Regis College, Toronto, in 1962, at Gonzaga University, Spokane, in 1963, at Georgetown University, Washington, in 1964, at Boston College in 1968 and 1970, at Regis College, Toronto, again in 1969; lectures at the Milltown Institute of Theology and Philosophy, Dublin, 1971, were based on the completed book.

60   Institute on The Method of Theology, Regis College, Toronto, 1962. Lonergan had his thought on interpretation well worked out by 1962; there is little difference between this lecture and ch. 7 of *Method* ten years later; no doubt ch. 17 of *Insight* gave him a head start.

61   Institute on The Method of Theology, Regis College, Toronto, 1962.

62   The Institute was held under the title 'Knowledge and learning', but Lonergan's very fundamental ideas could be reworked and included in almost any topic assigned him.

63   B. Lonergan, 'The mediation of Christ in prayer' (ed. M. Morelli), *Method: Journal of Lonergan Studies* 2/1 (March 1984), pp. 1–20. The editor has integrated two sources: Lonergan's own notes for lectures on mediation the preceding summer at Gonzaga University, Spokane, and a tape-recording of a lecture at Thomas More Institute, Montreal, on 24 September 1963, with the same title as the published article.

64   We have no tape-recording of this week of lectures on 'The method of theology', Georgetown University, Washington, July 1964, and the only record is the brief but invaluable set of notes (16pp.) made by Sister Rose Wilker.

65   The Wilker notes, p. 6.

66   Ibid., p. 7.

67   Ibid., pp. 9–10.

68   B. Lonergan, 'The subject' in *A Second Collection*, pp. 81–4.

69   I have drawn here on my own paper, 'An exploration of Lonergan's new notion of value', F. E. Crowe, *Appropriating the Lonergan Idea*, ed. M. Vertin (Washington, DC, 1989), pp. 52–5.

70   My own notes on the 1962 Institute on the Method of Theology, Regis College, Toronto, p. 9.

71   The notes of E. Martinez on the same Institute (from tape-recordings), tape 1, side 2, p. 11.

72   Ibid., p. 10. On the role of Dilthey, as attempting to do for historical sciences what Kant had done for natural sciences, see B. Lonergan in C. Going (ed.), *Dialogues in Celebration* (Montreal, 1980), pp. 291–5.

73   B. Lonergan in J. M. O'Hara (ed.), *Curiosity at the Center of One's Life: Statements and Questions of R. Eric O'Connor* (Montreal, 1984), p. 427.

74   B. Lonergan in E. Cahn and C. Going (eds), *The Question as Commitment: A Symposium* (Montreal, 1977), p. 103.

75   B. Lonergan, 'Belief: today's issue' in *A Second Collection*, p. 96.

76   B. Lonergan in J. M. O'Hara (ed.), *Curiosity at the Center*, p. 426.

77   B. Lonergan, '*Insight* revisited' in *A Second Collection*, p. 264: 'Dawson's *The Age of the Gods* introduced me to the anthropological notion of culture and so began the correction of my hitherto normative or classicist notion'.

78   B. Lonergan, *Caring*, p. 105, on his experience of teaching in Rome: 'I was learning all the time myself; I was moving into the European atmosphere in which phenomenology was dominant. There were highly trained students from Germany and France, Belgium and Northern Italy.'

79   See note 37 above.

5

The level of the times (II): *Instauratio Magna*

When *Method in Theology* was completed Lonergan could feel he had done his part in preparing the *Instauratio Magna*—the phrase is Bacon's, taken up by Kant—of Catholic learning which he had set out 45 years earlier to promote. True, for a while after the book was published in 1972, he did debate with himself whether he should return to his Christology and redo that topic in the way that his method would now suggest, but the debate ended with a decision for the alternative: to return rather to the economics on which he had worked in the 1930s and the 1940s, and see what he could do with that in the time that might still be given him—we have to remind ourselves that he could not count on the eleven years of working life that did in fact remain.

We must see *Method*, therefore, as a second rounding off and cutting short of a work in hand. As in 1953 he rounded off a preliminary study in the lifework he had planned, and cut it short, so now in 1972 he rounds off his lifework itself, and cuts short his contribution to the *Instauratio Magna* he saw as the need of our times. The difference is that 1953 was only an interruption of a task to which he returned, but 1972 marked the close of a lifelong effort; there would be a series of valuable papers and essays, but they would rather point to the work that remained than set about its achievement. The work he would do in economics would be significant, more so than his age and the state of his health gave hope for, but it was a limited foray into one of a hundred areas where praxis should follow theory, and lacked the comprehensive character of his effort in the previous 40 years.

Shall we say then that his early ambition was frustrated, that he did not succeed in bringing Catholic thought to the level of the times as he had hoped and struggled to do? In a way, yes, but in a more significant way, no.

He did not write the new theology that the level of the times seemed to call for; his contribution here, in its content, is quite modest in comparison with the bright dreams of the 1930s.[1] But to put the question that way is to distort in advance the answer. A chief part of his legacy is the realization that there is no definitive content for theology; it will vary from culture to culture, and even the uniformity it might achieve in a given culture is subject to change as generation succeeds generation. It became clear to him at an early stage that the kind of integration that Thomas Aquinas could at least envisage and in a measure achieve was no longer possible: far from mastering the whole of theology, one could not even be expert in the whole of the New Testament, but must take Paul or John or Luke as one's specialty.[2]

That, however, is a negative assessment of the level of our times and is to be complemented by its positive counterpart. Lonergan had no intention of critiquing an outdated scholasticism only to reduce theology to a kind of encyclopedic collection, stored in libraries and retrievable through indexes and computer searches. What remained? There was a third possibility, a middle way between a system carved in stone and the mountainous heap of positivist data: it was that of method. One could control the progress of learning in some degree through control of the process; one need not be at the mercy of superficial integration, or reduced to amassing 'facts' without meaning.

If then Lonergan's achievement in realized theology fell short of his dreams, in potential it far exceeded them, for it was in the nature of an organon, an instrument of human spirit, that with appropriate adjustments could be used far more widely than any such instrument previously conceived. The students of Aristotle collected his logical works into an instrument that came to be called an organon and controlled deductive thinking through the Middle Ages. Francis Bacon wrote of a *novum organum* that would perform a similar service for inductive thinking. Newman and his friend Robert William Hale exchanged ideas and hopes for a similar *novum organum* in the field of theology.[3] Lonergan's achievement was to construct the new organon that would be applicable in deduction or induction, in philosophy or theology, in the pursuit of any project in the field of human studies and human sciences, be it theoretical or practical, present or future, peculiar to one culture or to another—more briefly, in his own words, a method that 'would be relevant to any human studies that investigated a cultural past to guide its future'.[4] It was the only *Instauratio Magna* that the new level of the new times would allow, and it was this that was his achievement; his youthful dream was not frustrated.

But my purpose at the moment is not to evaluate his lifework and situate him in history. Something on that difficult question must be attempted in my final chapter, but the present purpose is to set forth the meaning of the achievement that *Method in Theology* was, and I begin as usual with a bit of history: the emergence of the organizing idea.

FEBRUARY 1965: BREAKTHROUGH TO FUNCTIONAL SPECIALTIES

The preceding chapter told the story of Lonergan's thinking on method, from an early interest as he was turning 22 at Heythrop College, through the years when it lay fallow, to the preliminary step of *Insight* and the various tentatives and piecemeal acquisitions of the 1950s and 1960s.

Throughout this time he was collecting materials, working out ideas, forming views, and storing it all in the hopper from which *Method* would emerge. The great breakthrough came in February 1965. We are inclined to dramatize this, likening it to Archimedes's 'Eureka' experience, and Lonergan did see it as a breakthrough after a slow build-up of forces and a long struggle with various ways of organizing them, but I do not think that he attached any special dramatic value to the experience. It was simply the last step in the long road and the steady plodding from *Insight* to *Method*: 'I started off with four functional specialties and then I added on a fifth and a sixth and so on. I had the eight, for the first time, in February of 1965.'[5]

It turned out that the road was not only long and plodding but held hidden perils. In February 1965 he began what was meant to be a year and a half free of teaching duties at the Gregorian University, a period that, in view of that early breakthrough, might have sufficed for writing his book. But in Canada, that first summer of his sabbatical, he went to his doctor for a routine check, and X-rays revealed a disturbing spot on his lungs. Tests showed the spot to be cancerous (he had been a smoker, though not a heavy one), and the right lung was removed. The wounds did not heal (he was subject to infection), and another operation was performed to collapse the chest wall. He was months recuperating and returning to work, and he never recovered the drive of previous years.[6]

The unspoken question during this melancholy time was always whether the surgery had removed all the cancerous growth. It had done so in fact (the cancer of the colon which forced another operation in 1982 was, it seems, an unconnected outbreak), but one could not know that before five years had elapsed, and it was just during those five years, working in the shadow of this threat, that he wrote *Method in Theology*, and sent it off to Darton, Longman & Todd in 1971.

Critics have found the book to lack the rigour of *Insight*. I disagree with that judgement, though I think I see the reasons for it. For one thing, where *Insight* made mathematics and the natural sciences the favoured arena for wrestling with intentionality analysis, *Method* takes the human sciences and human studies as the field for a similar struggle (a new Dilthey, perhaps, complementing a new Kant), and matters of the spirit will always seem less subject to rigorous analysis than those of the infrahuman world. In a phrase Lonergan would quote from Pascal, the heart has reasons that reason does not know, reasons that must be discussed with another standard of rigour. As we can learn from Aristotle, there is a difference, when we come to reason, between ethics and mathematics. But each one has its laws, and *Method* does not fail us in respect to its own proper standard of rigour.

Nevertheless, *Method* does suffer in comparison with *Insight*. It is schematic in style almost to the point of being laconic, and the content lacks the leisurely sweep of its great predecessor. This is especially apparent in the background chapters, where the categories are developed that will be employed in the functional specialties of theology. Thus, we have a chapter on transcendental method to give 'the basic anthropological component' of theological method, a chapter on religion to 'supply the specifically religious component', and in between chapters on the human good and human meaning to allow us to speak with authority on religion.[7] These four chapters are packed with thought, but one feels that the Lonergan of pre-surgery times would have greatly expanded them, perhaps devoting separate chapters to categories for research and history, as he did for interpretation (ch. 3) and dialectic (ch. 2), as well as a chapter to show how transcendental method operates descending through the four levels, and not just in the ascent from experience to value. The elements of such expansion are not lacking; the rigorous reduction to basic categories is not lacking; what is lacking, I feel, is the extensive treatment to which *Insight* had accustomed us.

The high point of the background section and the heart of the book is chapter 5 on the functional specialties. To be noted at once: we are dealing with *specialties*, and with specialties in the theoretic pattern, in the universe of thought. Lonergan has no objection to catechetics, and indeed, as his final chapter (communications) shows, the whole volume reaches its goal in the applications of which catechetics is an important part. Again, Lonergan has no objection to prayer and worship: 'Man's response to transcendent mystery is adoration'; but one need not stop there: 'adoration does not exclude words', and words lead to theology.[8] Lonergan was not a liturgist, nor a catechist, nor a poet, nor a musician, nor a journalist, nor an ecclesiastical diplomat—all of them of course performing necessary and valuable functions—he was a theologian, and it was method in theological specialization that concerned him.

The first question intrinsic to chapter 5 centres on the specialties as functional. The eight specialties and their structure have become so familiar that we are apt to overlook this important preliminary. Before we begin to structure the functions, we have to choose *them*, rather than fields or departments, as the principle of division and the structuring idea. For the rain-forest growth of modern thought requires specialization, but on what principle shall we divide? That is a very basic question.

Thus one could specialize, and we do, by dividing and subdividing the field of data: field specialization. Then you get specialists in Scripture, who subdivide, first, into Old Testament and New Testament scholars. The latter then subdivide into specialists on the Gospels, on Paul, on the Apocalypse, and so on, and these tend to subdivide again and again. All this is very necessary, but it provides no way of integrating these various fields into a unified account of theology.

Another option is to specialize by dividing and subdividing departments (we could say subjects, but that word so often means the human agent now that its use here would be confusing). Here we divide and subdivide, not the field of data, but the results of investigations. The former was a division into material parts, the latter is a division by conceptual classification. Thus, human studies divide into biological, neurological, psychic, and so on; and religious studies, say in the Old Testament, divide into 'semitic languages,

Hebrew history, the religions of the ancient Near East, and Christian theology'.[9] Here it is easy to achieve some kind of unified picture, if only by a device like the classification by means of dichotomy in Porphyry's tree: being, material being, living material, vegetative living, and so on. It is less easy to achieve agreement on the unification, or to see how useful it would be if you did get agreement.

Lonergan's division is not by data to be investigated and not by results of the investigations, but by distinguishing stages or functions in the process from data to results. Thus, the same New Testament data come under consideration whether you are a textual critic, an interpreter, or a historian; but the three scholars indicated are at different stages in the study of the data, and perform different functions in regard to them. This feature of Lonergan's work is not studied as much as the structure and content of the specialties are.

Still the structure is crucial; it is the channel that will direct the stream. It is more, however, than *mere* structure; Lonergan had said in his 1958 lectures: 'with regard to the content of heuristic structure, the expression is ambiguous. The heuristic structure in itself is a content . . . But further by the content of the heuristic structure you also mean what fills in this structure.'[10] That is, there is a material content, and what we might call an operational content. This suggests two questions to ask of *Method*, one on the structure and its content as structure, and the other on the content that fills the structure. The latter is theology proper; there is a series of particular theologies that one may choose, and the task of writing them is endless. It is the former that is our interest.

FUNCTIONS AND STRUCTURE

The structure, then, derives from the four levels of consciousness to be found through self-appropriation; they correspond to the three words *what*, *is* and *ought*, that arise in succession after the presentations on a first level of sense and consciousness. *What* does it mean? *Is* my idea the right one? The situation then being what it is, what *ought* I to do? These questions, with the level of presentations, make the four levels now so familiar that no exposition is needed here.

There was, however, what I consider his most important later addition, making explicit what was very close to formulation in *Method*: the two directions in which one might move along the structure. There is the way up from the presentations of experience, through ideas and judgements, to values and responsible action; one might call this the way of achievement, of self-taught learning, of progress for the human race. And there is the way down through values handed on in family and society, judgements imbibed in a community of love rather than formed in personal acquisition, understanding that comes tardily to the support of this set of judgements, and the experience made mature and perceptive as a result; one might call this the way of tradition, of heritage, of learning by osmosis, of handing on what previous generations had achieved.[11]

This second direction has not been exploited. Lonergan himself came late to its formulation; we do not find it, where it belongs, in the background chapters of *Method*, but in those post-*Method* papers which point a way but do not follow it to the end. Though he left clues, which hindsight can now discover, in his earlier writings, it was only in papers and essays between 1974 and 1977 that he spoke explicitly of this second direction. He did so on one occasion after another, and there is a clear sense of something new here, but it was never the central theme of any of those papers and he did not develop it with anything like the thoroughness of the upward movement from experience to responsibility.

From the structure of consciousness we move to the specialties they organize. The four levels, and the two directions in which one may move through them, give the eight functional specialties. We collect data in research, and begin to classify and organize them. We determine their meaning in interpretation. There is a succession of interpretations, and resulting developments in human institutions, which we study in history. This necessitates study of the different horizons which are the source, in the researchers and interpreters and historians, of differences in the data we seek, the meanings we give them, the histories we write; and this study, undertaken in dialectic, brings us squarely to the question of our own involvement, to our choice of a horizon that will be 'the fertile source of further knowledge and care', though it is also the boundary that will 'limit our capacities for assimilating more than we already have attained'.[12]

The first three specialties left us comfortably on the side of positive work, not taking a stand but talking about the stand taken by others, discourse *in oratione obliqua*. The discomfort of a need to choose appears in the fourth specialty. The choice we make is inevitably a function of what we are; as the Middle Ages repeated after Aristotle, 'Qualis unusquisque est, talis et finis videtur ei': 'the end appears to each man in a form answering to his character'.[13] If we are not what we should be, and the supposition is that we are never quite that, there will be need of conversion, in fact of a series of conversions. With this we are effectively transferred from discourse *in oratione obliqua* to discourse *in oratione recta*: we must become personally involved, laying our own foundations, affirming our own positions, understanding them in our own systems, communicating with others in the intersubjectivity of our own situation.

Thus, on the four levels of the upward development of consciousness we have research corresponding to experience, interpretation corresponding to understanding, history corresponding to judgement, and dialectic corresponding to decision. And, on the same four levels but in a downward movement, we have foundations, doctrines, systematics, and communications on the levels, respectively, of decision, judgement, understanding, and experience.

FUNCTIONS AND CONTENT: RESEARCH, INTERPRETATION, HISTORY

The structure of human consciousness discovered in intentionality analysis and the unity this makes possible in the disparate work of researchers, exegetes, historians, controversialists and apologists, magisterial and systematic workers, preachers and missionaries—all this constitutes one of Lonergan's major contributions to theology. But *how* is that unity made possible? The structure would be useless unless there were found a way to utilize it, to relate it to those sprawling results of modern scholarship and thought. I have spoken as if there were an obvious relation of research and communications to the first level, of interpretation and systematics to the second, and so on. But in fact the relation is not quite so obvious; there is a mediating factor, and it is content.

This is not the content that fills the structure, but rather the content I have called operational. What fills the structure is a material content that grows and grows till libraries and museums overflow, and computer storage capacity is forced into continual expansion. That is not, and cannot be, the topic of discussion here. But there is a content proper to each level of consciousness that relates it to the type of object studied in each functional specialty; it regards the *genus* of the content, the *type* of knowledge involved, the *kind* of specialization needed for each of the eight functions;

that operational content is the mediating factor, and our present concern.

Two preliminary points may help. First, we should rid ourselves in advance of a useless difficulty: that of conceiving a specialty exclusively in terms of its proper activity. To declare the operation of a certain level of consciousness proper to a particular specialty does not exclude specialists from operating on the other levels; in fact, they must operate on them as well:

> So the textual critic will select the method (level of decision) that he feels will lead to the discovery (level of understanding) of what one may reasonably affirm (level of judgment) was written in the original text (level of experience). The textual critic, then, operates on all four levels, but his goal is the end proper to the first level, namely, to ascertain the data.[14]

The other point is positive, though only an analogy. It is the parallel, that I find useful, of the lawcourt. Here there are four distinct but related operations, with parts played by four distinct participants. Witnesses provide the data: what they saw, heard, and so on. Lawyers provide the interpretation, in fact, two contrary interpretations, one for the defence, another for the prosecution. The jury makes the judgement of fact: the defendant is or is not guilty. The judge evaluates the whole process and takes appropriate action in consequence. Now what the millions of witnesses in the history of law have said is certainly a content of that level, however difficult it is to collect and however useless when it is collected; but what the role of witnessing is, what the limits of its function, and so on—that is content in another sense, and it is the content, I suppose, that a theory of lawcourts would study. Something analogous will obtain in our theory of theological method.

With these preliminaries we come to the general content, as distinct from the material content, proper to each specialty. Thus, the material content of research is every single datum, in the form of writings, inscriptions, monuments, artefacts, that is relevant to any branch whatever of theology. Is anything excluded under that heading? When we have acquired the hundreds of volumes of Migne's Greek and Latin patrologies, we have only begun to collect the data in just one of the many departments of theology. What is wanted here is something much more general as an idea, and therefore much less space-consuming in its expression. From this viewpoint the content of research is not, say, a particular variant in manuscript readings; it is data as data. What do we mean by data? What role do they play in the theological enterprise? How do we collect, classify, store, and retrieve them? How do they relate, for example, to dogma?—A question whose relevance is seen as soon as an atheist scholar and a believing exegete read together a text of Scripture.

Lonergan did not give much attention to research in his book on theological method—a bare two pages. Nor does he list even in general the categories proper to research. What he does do is more general even than general categories: he relates the work of research to cognitional process: 'research is an enormously diversified category and doing research is much more a matter of practice than of theory . . . [It] is always a concrete task that is guided not by abstract generalities but by the practical intelligence generated by the self-correcting process of learning.'[15] From this perspective it becomes clear that one cannot specify categories for research; one goes rather to a master and becomes an apprentice. Nevertheless, more could have been said, had Lonergan written *Method* in the style of *Insight*, and later he admitted with some regret, 'I fear that my book did not emphasize enough the importance of research'.[16]

Interpretation fares better. Its goal is understanding what was meant, and meaning had been a topic in the *verbum* articles of 1946–49, had engaged Lonergan's attention in chapter 17 of *Insight*, and became a focal point in his lectures of the early 1960s, through the influence, it seems, of authors like Dilthey. The basic affirmation, and the one that relates interpretation properly to the second level of consciousness, is that interpretation *understands* what is meant. Again the material content is unmanageably vast: any meaning whatever that can be given to any item whatever in the list of data that research collects. But the content of interpretation as part of a heuristic structure deals with categories like stages and realms of meaning, modes and levels of thought and expression, the circumstances and intention of the writer, historical context, and so on; and of course with cognitional theory, epistemology and metaphysics, which for Lonergan are ever present under the surface.[17]

While interpretation is rather easily related to the second level, and its heuristic content spelled out accordingly, it is not so obvious that history finds its special goal on the third level, that it is in sequence to interpretation, that the categories which specify its heuristic content are related most properly to those of judgement, the third level of consciousness—Lonergan's position here has in fact been vigorously questioned.

To see the matter from his viewpoint, we first remember that we are dealing with the specialized area of theology, that Lonergan's own theology was Christian, that Christianity is a historical religion with origins in the past, that the past comes down to us largely in written documents, that the documents can be studied with ever new techniques from ever changing perspectives. Theology therefore, and especially Christian theology, inevitably has a history of interpretation.

This does not, however, answer the question why history is especially related to the third level of consciousness. So secondly, though history, if it is to be linked with the third level, must concern the real, still the reality in question need not be the reality presented in revelation, 'the substance of things hoped for'; there must be a function of theology to deal with this, but we have it in *doctrines* which, like history, is a specialty on the third level. But doctrines deal with reality in mediated theology and *in oratione recta*, while history remains *in oratione obliqua* and in mediating theology: the history and sequence of what the Church has believed, and of the resulting institutions. History as a specialty asks what happened between 1 Thessalonians, where Paul says next to nothing on the relation of law and grace, and Galatians, where he cannot stop talking about it, or what happened between the New Testament and the Council of Nicaea to require, after three centuries, the intrusion of the term *homoousion* into Christian belief.

This distinction and relation of the two functions of history and doctrines, with both pertaining to the third level and each in its own way related to the real, but one in mediating theology, the other in mediated theology—this, I think, must have been a most satisfying insight for Lonergan. His whole work in theology, we reported him as saying, was to introduce history into Catholic theology. The distinction and relation of mediating and mediated theology did not give him automatic answers to all the questions that arose and were studied—on the 'chasm', the 'impenetrable wall' between theology and its sources, on the permanence of truth, on transposition from one cultural expression to another—but it provided a basic structure in which those questions could be raised, distinguished, and related to one another, and in which the possibility of a solution might emerge.

FUNCTIONS AND CONTENT: DIALECTIC, FOUNDATIONS

How do we move from mediating theology to mediated? With this question we come to a very innovative contribution Lonergan made to theological method, the insertion of dialectic and foundations between the empirical work of the scholar and the committed position of the believer.

There was something analogous in the old apologetics, but the difference is greater than the similarity. Apologetics was a matter of proof. You proved your position step by step:

> A natural theology established the existence of God. A natural ethics established the obligation of worshiping God. The prophecies of the Old Testament and the miracles of the New established the divine origin of the Christian religion, and the Christian message settled the identity of the true Church.[18]

From that point on everything was plain sailing.

It was all very logical. It proved everything. And it convinced nobody. For what we will admit, what will convince us, what will have meaning for us, is a matter of the horizon which enters constitutively into our knowing and caring, but also limits our interests and judgements. If something lies outside our horizon, we dismiss it as irrelevant or perhaps nonsense, meaningless; if the question of enlarging our horizon becomes serious, the experience is traumatic. It is here that the function of dialectic finds its place: dialectic analyses horizons, their limitations, and the possibility of enlarging them; it also challenges us, through conversion, to achieve that enlargement.

Dialectic, then, raises the question of conversion as an existential one calling for decision. Foundations goes further; it supposes that we have taken that existential step, and it transfers the theologian from academic mediating theology, in which we study what someone said or what happened in the Church, to the commitment of a mediated theology, in which we take our own position, affirm our own beliefs, wrestle with their meaning and coherence, and hand them on to others.

We must return here to a work noted but not examined in Chapter 4: Lonergan's 1967 lecture on 'The new context of theology', published under the title 'Theology in its new context'. It is a turning point in his thinking on the new foundations needed for a new theology on the level of the times. The old, while true enough, are no longer appropriate:

> One type of foundation suits a theology that aims at being deductive, static, abstract, universal, equally applicable to all places and to all times. A quite different foundation is needed when theology turns from deductivism to an empirical approach, from the static to the dynamic, from the abstract to the concrete, from the universal to the historical totality of particulars, from invariable rules to intelligent adjustment and adaptation.[19]

For his new foundation Lonergan looks to conversion:

> It is to consist not in objective statement, but in subjective reality. The objective statements of a *de vera religione*, *de Christo legato*, *de ecclesia*, *de inspiratione scripturae*, *de locis theologicis*, are as much in need of a foundation as are those of other tracts. But behind all statements is the stating subject. What is normative and foundational for subjects stating theology is to be found, I have suggested, in reflection on conversion, where conversion is taken as an ongoing process, concrete and dynamic, personal, communal, and historical.[20]

FUNCTIONS AND CONTENT: DOCTRINES, SYSTEMATICS, COMMUNICATIONS

The sequence of the remaining three functional specialties, and their relation to one another, are close enough to the sequence and relation of their predecessors—revealed *truth*, of which we seek *understanding*, in order to *preach* sound doctrine—as not to require even that sketchy exposition I have given the first five. It will be more useful, I think, to consider some of the particular questions that arise with regard to them.

With regard to *doctrines* the crucial question for many is the transfer of truth from culture to culture, its permanence in the various transpositions it has undergone in the course of the Christian centuries. We have seen that this question arose only with the discovery of human historicity in the last two centuries, that it was not a mediaeval problem, that Thomas Aquinas could go from Aristotle to Scripture and back again with little sense of dislocation.

It became a question, however, for Newman, and so he wrote *An Essay on the Development of Christian Doctrine* (1845). It is an even more disturbing question in our time, with our sense of a pluralism of cultures that did not, I think, pose as sharp a question for Newman.

Lonergan laboured long and resolutely to understand both the gap between cultures and the way truth can be transposed from culture to culture, but what he has to say under these headings is always to be understood in the context of a much more fundamental question on the nature of truth itself, and will be perpetually misunderstood if that context is lacking. This is the topic on which I would say a word now.

Lonergan had never the slightest doubt, so far as I can discover, of the element of truth in divine revelation and in our reception of revelation. God entered a human world characterized by the levels of experience, understanding, truth, and value; God entered our world at all levels and did not, quite inexplicably, skip the third. For the first level there are data of experience on Jesus Christ and there are data of experience on the indwelling Spirit; for the fourth there is the attraction of the incarnate Word that led the disciples to leave all things and follow him, and there is the love of God flooding our hearts through the Spirit who is given to us; in between for the second level there is the effort, not without success, to understand the meaning of Jesus, and the effort, not without success, to discern the meaning the indwelling Spirit would convey to us. Why, when the first, fourth and second levels of consciousness are addressed in revelation, should God exclude the third? Or, to put it more coarsely, why should truth be a dirty word for theologians?

The reason, I suggest, is that theologians by and large do not know what to do with truth, or how to find its foundations. They are still victims of a philosophy that two centuries ago established a Copernican revolution, but did not succeed in probing truth the way it probed understanding. Furthermore, they are mesmerized by a history that relativizes formulations and doctrines so completely, it seems, as to defy all our efforts to assign them foundations. What are they to do, except perhaps take refuge in the love that moves the sun and all the stars and in the symbols that appeal to our psyche, while they devote their systematic study to religious language instead of to religious truth?

That Lonergan established the virtually unconditioned as constitutive of human knowing is a first principle in the study of his achievement. We have seen the relevance of this to the critical problem that arises as soon as we realize that knowing is based on insight and not on taking a good look. We have now to add its relevance to the transmission of truth, and the permanence of meaning that can remain despite the greatest variety in expression. It is only when we get hold of what happens in insight that we can appreciate the role of the virtually unconditioned for both the establishment of truth and its transmission. For the content of insight is not a datum; it is an intelligibility. It is without words or language. It is prior to language; it can endure though language changes. The interior word, Augustine liked to say, 'is neither Greek nor Latin, nor any other language'.[21] To understand this, he adds, we must 'get hold of a word . . . not only before it is sounded, but even before the images of its sounds are revolved in fantasy [*cogitatione*]'.[22] What we have here is the counterpart of the point on the real that Lonergan made so emphatically: Augustine's discovery that the 'real' need not be a 'body'.[23] What is the source of this 'spiritual' character of the interior word? It is the 'spiritual' character of insight, which is prior to inner word and much more to the spoken word. This is as operative in the transmission of truth as it is in its first acquisition.

With such an understanding of understanding, of truth, of the handing on of truth, one is not really thwarted by the changing expressions of doctrine. There is a problem of how to follow their sequence, how to understand the transition—this is the point of Lonergan's study of the stages of meaning, of the differentiations of consciousness, of the brands of common sense, of transpositions from culture to culture, and so on. But the permanence of meaning ceases to be the utter mystery that it has to be for those who make language primary. This philosophy of truth and its transmission has then to be put to the service of religious truth and theology— analogously, of course, for always in theology we have the element of mystery.

The next function of theology to consider is *systematics*, which, of all eight specialties, is closest to its counterpart in Lonergan's scholastic theology. The continuity is indicated in the fact that, though systematics is his area *par excellence*, his chapter on that topic is one of the shortest in the book;[24] it is made explicit in the statement, 'I am not proposing any novelty. I am proposing a return to the type of systematic theology illustrated by Aquinas' *Summa contra Gentiles* and *Summa theologiae*.'[25]

Still, there are differences. For one thing, systematics is related now to religious experience, not just to revealed truths; hence, 'an orientation to transcendent mystery is basic to systematic theology.

It provides the primary and fundamental meaning of the name, God.'[26] For another, there is at this time the development that we noted earlier in the very notion of system; in lectures given the year of *Method*'s publication, Lonergan urged that the general characteristics of a system 'may be found in quite different contexts . . . there is the Aristotelian type based on a metaphysics; there is the modern type based on empirical science; there is the transcendental type based on intentionality analysis'.[27] This last type was a radical change: 'Modern philosophy entailed a radical shift in systematic thinking'.[28] But perhaps enough has been said to indicate the continuity and the development from scholasticism to methodical systematics.

The last of the functional specialties, the goal to which the preceding seven lead, is *communications*. Like research, its first-level counterpart in mediating theology, it is so diffuse as to exclude any comprehensive statement of its content; as every datum of the past millennia and the present day is potential material for research, so every human being at any place, time, or culture, is the potential recipient of the good news in communications. How is one to describe a specialty that would deal with such a multiplicity? Obviously, only in the most general terms; so Lonergan's chapters on research and communications are the two shortest in the book.

In some sense, communication has been the concern of theology from its beginnings, as it was the concern of the apostles before theology began. What has always been needed is the expression of the good news in a way that reaches the recipient, with the fidelity to Tradition that ensures it is really the good news, and not some watering down or counterfeit. What Lonergan would contribute, in the context of his own ideas and method, is achieved through the merging of a crosscultural base with 'an accurate and intimate understanding of the culture and the language of the people' addressed,[29] and the crosscultural base is, of course, the self that is given and operative before we talk about it or achieve any degree of self-appropriation.

This is now a familiar idea, close to the heart of what Lonergan has to say on any topic. But we must note that his application of the idea in this field underwent considerable development before he came to its final formulation. The 1954 paper, 'Theology and understanding', which I would take as marking the high point of his scholastic period and at the same time giving a glimpse of new horizons, still speaks of communications as a fairly automatic result of systematic understanding of theology. The synthetic view 'simplifies and enriches one's own spiritual life, and it bestows upon one's teaching the enviable combination of sureness of doctrine with versatility of expression'. Further, it remains

> for it is fixed upon one's intellectual memory. So we find that non-Catholic clergymen, often more learned in scripture and the fathers, preach from their pulpits the ideas put forward in the latest stimulating book or article, while the Catholic priest, often burdened with sacerdotal duties and administrative tasks, spontaneously expounds the epistle or gospel of the Sunday in the light of an understanding that is common to the ages.[30]

Lonergan had quite early seen the 'chasm' between Scripture and theological understanding; he was slower, we have noted, to see the similar chasm between theological understanding and the hearers here and now of the word. But the latter chasm presents the same problem in reverse; where the historian has to bridge the first gap to achieve understanding, the preacher has to bridge the second to communicate it. This is the problem not sufficiently adverted to in 'Theology and understanding', taken up now in the eighth functional specialty.

THE NEW LEVEL OF THE TIMES

How different the view of theology supposed in this method is from the standard conception of theology as *fides quaerens intellectum*, faith seeking understanding. That latter formulation was limited to two of the eight functional specialties: faith regarded *doctrines* derived from Scripture and Tradition and taught by the Church; theology regarded the understanding of these doctrines in *systematics*. There is now an enormous expansion, 'a greatly enlarged notion of theology'; it no longer consists merely of doctrines and systematics, with research, interpretation, history, dialectic, foundations, and communications somehow stuck on; these latter areas are now intrinsic to theology; now 'there pertain to theology investigations that otherwise have to be conceived as auxiliary disciplines, e.g., textual criticism'.[31]

The enlargement is not just a matter of having eight functions instead of two. There are more fundamental factors that underlie this mere numerical expansion. There is one first of all on the empirical side:

theology was a deductive, and it has become largely an empirical science. It was a deductive science in the sense that its theses were conclusions to be proven from the premisses provided by Scripture and Tradition. It has become an empirical science in the sense that Scripture and Tradition now supply not premisses, but data.[32]

These data are assembled in research, their meaning is studied in interpretation, with the sequence of interpretations yielding history —all of them matters of empirical inquiry.

There is another and, in my opinion, still more important factor in the enlargement: the insertion of dialectic and foundations between the empirical functions of the scholar and the committed functions of the believer, and the role of conversion in effecting the transition from the empirical to the committed, from mediating to mediated theology. We had a long tradition, of course, relating theology to the holiness of the theologian. But the holiness remained extrinsic to the theology; now what a theologian is becomes intrinsic to his theological operations: 'Where formerly a discipline was specifically theological because it dealt with revealed truths, now it is authentically theological because the theologian has been converted intellectually, morally, and religiously'.[33]

We may note also that the enlargement resulting from these factors does not stop with the addition of new specialties; there is enlargement also within the specialties, more accurately within the areas that in previous theology corresponded to the specialties. Thus for apologetics, there is the role of dialectic as a generalized apologetic;[34] for doctrines, the various distinct notions set out at the start of chapter 12; for preaching (communications), the interdisciplinary factor.[35]

The net result is a theology that fulfils the function Lonergan assigns it in the first line of his Introduction to *Method in Theology*: 'A theology mediates between a cultural matrix and the significance and role of a religion in that matrix';[36] a theology, in other words, that responds to Lonergan's lifelong pursuit, one that speaks with authority to its time and on the level of its time.

Notes

1   The papers Lonergan produced in the decade following publication of *Method* are 'sleepers'—important for clarifying his thought and carrying it forward, but as yet largely unnoticed. They are not, however, exercises in the theology that *Method* calls for and makes possible; one

paper that might raise hopes in this direction, 'Christology today: methodological reflections', is largely what its title asserts it to be, a discussion of method; see B. Lonergan in *A Second Collection*, ed. W. Ryan and B. Tyrrell (London/Philadelphia, 1974/1975), pp. 74–99.

2   Of course, Thomas too was handicapped in his own way by lack of specialized resources; witness his remark as he looked on the beauty of Paris: 'I'd sooner have available Chrysostom's commentary on Matthew'. See M.-D. Chenu, *Introduction à l'étude de saint Thomas d'Aquin* (Montreal/Paris, 1954), p. 211 n. 1.

3   C. Dessain and T. Gornall (eds), *The Letters and Diaries of John Henry Newman* (Oxford, 1973), pp. 56–7.

4   B. Lonergan, 'Bernard Lonergan responds' in P. McShane (ed.), *Foundations of Theology* (Dublin/London, 1971), p. 233. See also P. Lambert, C. Tansey and C. Going (eds), *Caring about Meaning: Patterns in the Life of Bernard Lonergan* (Montreal, 1982), p. 57: the specialties are not applicable to mathematics, but are applicable to 'anything human that draws upon the past to enlighten the future'. In 1969, asked for an article, Lonergan sent 'Functional specialties' (now ch. 5 in *Method*) to *Gregorianum*; the title was changed editorially to 'Functional specialties in theology', a change Lonergan accepted without fuss but unwisely, for it gave a handle to the criticism that he was offering as method in theology what was not specifically theological. Ch. 5, we remember, is part of the 'Background' chapters in the book, not the theological 'Foreground'; it provides *general* categories that other disciplines besides theology may use.

5   *Caring*, p. 59.

6   A letter to G. Sala, 19 September 1966, shows the concern he had felt about resuming public speaking: 'I read the "Quamquam" here for the beginning of the school year [traditional lecture with this Ciceronian opening] and was greatly relieved to observe that it caused no shortage of breath so, with due care, my speaking voice should be all right'. (From the letter kindly provided by Fr Sala.)

7   B. Lonergan, *Method in Theology* (London/New York, 1972), p. 25.

8   Ibid., p. 344. Note that there is, in scientific procedures, a reversal of the priorities of everyday life; in the latter one descends from the level of affectivity through the four levels; the scientists' procedure is the opposite: assemble the data, interpret their meaning, come to a judgement, and act responsibly on that knowledge.

9   *Method*, p. 126.

10 *Understanding and Being: The Halifax Lectures on* Insight, ed. E. Morelli and M. Morelli (2nd edn; *Collected Works of Bernard Lonergan* 5, Toronto, 1990), p. 341.

11 For an early, though not the earliest account of these two contrasting movements, see B. Lonergan, 'Healing and creating in history' in *A Third Collection*, ed. F.E. Crowe (New York/London, 1985), p. 106.

12 *Method*, p. 237.

13 Aristotle, *Nicomachean Ethics*, Bk III, ch. 5, 1114a 30f., Ross translation. For Thomist use of the principle see, for example, *Summa Theologiae* Ia, q. 83, a. 1, obj. 5a; Ia IIa, q. 10, a. 3, obj. 2a.

14 *Method*, p. 134.
15 Ibid., p. 149.
16 B. Lonergan, letter to F. Crowe, 3 March 1980.
17 *Method*, p. 127.
18 B. Lonergan, 'Variations in fundamental theology', unpublished lecture (Trinity College, Toronto, 13 November 1973), p. 4.
19 B. Lonergan, 'Theology in its new context' in *A Second Collection*, pp. 63–4 (see Chapter 4, note 57 above).
20 Ibid., p. 67.
21 Augustine, *De Trinitate*, Bk XV, cap. 10, n. 19.
22 Ibid.
23 B. Lonergan, *Insight: A Study of Human Understanding* (2nd edn; London/New York, 1958), pp. xx–xxi, xxiii, 412.
24 Nineteen pages; only two chapters are shorter, both in the nature of the case: Research, and Communications.
25 B. Lonergan, *Method*, pp. 339–40.
26 Ibid., p. 341—a pregnant statement that would certainly be on my short list if I were asked for one-liners to indicate what Lonergan is up to in theology.
27 B. Lonergan, *Philosophy of God, and Theology: The Relationship between Philosophy of God and the Functional Specialty, Systematics* (St Michael's Lectures, Gonzaga University, Spokane, 1972; London/Philadelphia, 1973), p. 6.
28 B. Lonergan, *Method*, p. 345.
29 Ibid., p. 362.
30 B. Lonergan, 'Theology and understanding' in *Collection*, ed. F. E. Crowe and R. M. Doran (2nd edn; *Collected Works of Bernard Lonergan* 4, Toronto, 1988), p. 125.
31 B. Lonergan, 'Bernard Lonergan responds' in P. McShane (ed.), *Foundations of Theology*, p. 224.
32 B. Lonergan, 'Theology in its new context' in *A Second Collection*, p. 58.
33 B. Lonergan, 'Bernard Lonergan responds' in P. McShane (ed.), *Foundations of Theology*, p. 224. This 'response' is invaluable in its explanation of what *Method* is all about; in effect, like '*Insight* revisited', it is a review-article on his own book, only this time the 'review' preceded the book by a couple of years—the response belongs to the Lonergan congress of 1970, *Method* came out only in 1972.
34 B. Lonergan, *Method*, p. 130.
35 Ibid., p. 132, and see pp. 364–7.
36 Ibid., p. xi.

6

From the level of the times to the future

Forty years ago a French Jesuit, fellow-student of mine in Rome, asked me 'What is Lonergan's *apport*?' It was not easy to answer that question then; it is not easy even now. It will be impossible, I think, to do so in a definitive way till new generations come on the scene, but the condition of a definitive answer is a series of answers that are not definitive, and one must start the series somewhere. So I will do what I can with the question. A second question linked with this, one that I ask myself with even less hope of saying the last word, regards the future of what is being called the Lonergan movement: did it peak with his own work of 1957—he hasn't had an idea since *Insight*, one critic remarked—or, as some of us believe, is its time still to come? These questions, with concluding reflections, will structure our final chapter.

LONERGAN'S CONTRIBUTION (1): CONCEPTUALITY

In this tentative view of Lonergan's *apport* I would go back to a notion mentioned in Chapter 2, his *Begrifflichkeit*, his conceptuality, the set of organized concepts with which he approaches a problem. It is a simple way to introduce the question of his contribution, though I would not say it goes to the heart of the matter. Still, I find it illuminating just to run through the subtitles of any standard work of scholasticism, and compare the results with the data from a similar exercise in Lonergan, especially in his later writings.

From the first exercise, we can list in helter-skelter fashion such headings as these: act and potency, immanent and transitive action, analogical knowledge of God, substance and accident, subsistence, *in esse* and *in fieri*, essence and existence, proper object of intellect, necessary truths, natural theology, virtues and habits, faculties of the soul, intellect and will, universal concepts, syllogisms, induction and deduction, intellection, certitude, the transcendentals, principles of being, matter and form, speculative and practical, union of soul and body, eternal law.

When we turn to Lonergan, we may find many of the terms just listed, but a more characteristic list would be something like the following: dynamism and being, problem and solution, question and answer, research and classification, description and explanation, classical and statistical science, aesthetic and dramatic patterns of experience, heuristic and determinate concepts, models and categories, development from above and development from below, structures and content, hermeneutic of suspicion and hermeneutic of retrieval, hypotheses and probabilities, horizons and biases, community and alienation, genetic and dialectic, the authentic and the inauthentic, meaning and value, nature and history, stages and breakdowns, progress and decline, cultural and religious, differentiations and integrations, drifting and conversion, pluralism and the transcultural, naive and critical realism, interiority and extroversion, belief and religious experience, and so on.

Clearly a new world of thought has emerged, and the level of the times is characterized by a new *Begrifflichkeit*. It is not that Lonergan repudiated the scholastic terms; many of them he used himself in his earlier years, though with his own creative understanding of their meaning. Neither is it the case that he invented the terms in the new modes of thought; many of them he took over from current usage, though giving them again his own personal content. But the list will orient us in our effort to follow Lonergan's contribution.

LONERGAN'S CONTRIBUTION (2): INTEGRATION

A second step brings us closer, I feel, to Lonergan's distinctive *apport*: his organization of the categories, the integral character of his thinking. The integrating power is exercised not only with regard to any particular set of categories, but also with regard to the sets that succeed one another in history and constitute so much of its continuity/discontinuity.

It is there that the fundamental character of his thinking is especially evident. His students will remember how often his lectures would take them back to what is fundamental. By this he did not mean some fundamental concept, not even the concept of being; he meant the very dynamism itself of the questioning, thinking, formulating, testing, judging, evaluating human consciousness, restlessly seeking fulfilment in the intelligible, the true, the real, the good, the holy. Further, he saw this principle, this immanent dynamism of human consciousness, as functioning in time and over time, operating in authentic or inauthentic fashion, differentiating itself in myriad ways, relating those ways to one another, maybe genetically, maybe dialectically, through the immanent source of them all.

A good index of this integrating power at work is the critical foundation he was able to give his metaphysics: from the metaphysics latent in our very use of the word 'is' he could move through self-appropriation to the traditional metaphysics of Thomas Aquinas; it is not searching in a dark room for a black object that is not there, but right out in the open as the consequence of the way all of us notice and observe, question and form ideas, test and judge. The same principle is at work in the way he could take over the metaphysics of scholasticism, with its potency–form–act in both the substantial and accidental orders, rethink these orders, in terms more in tune with the correlations of science, as central and conjugate, and make this rather static metaphysics dynamic through the addition of a new set of potency–form–act, one that takes account of a universe functioning through emergent probability and issuing in genera and species in a developmental process.

Another index can be noted by turning to a broader view of history. If we travel across the centuries in the seven-league boots of the summarizer, we may see Plato as representing the intellectual principle, Thomas Aquinas as representing the judgemental principle (adding *esse* to form), and Kierkegaard as representing the principle of responsibility and involvement. What is needed at the end of the twentieth century is a power of integration that can hold all three principles in intrinsic relation to one another, and that is what Lonergan's intentionality analysis attempts to do.

The mention of Kierkegaard reminds us of the need for an integrating power also in the rather special and very important area of system and history, for system requires strict generalization, and history resists generalization quite stubbornly. The liberating key is the act of insight or understanding, which always occurs with regard to the particular, but is virtually universal and when fully in our possession yields the universal concept, from which we proceed to system.

I believe also that the organon Lonergan constructed makes easily possible what others have found so difficult, the union of the transcendental and the historical. For it is a structure that allows for infinite variety in the content. Thus we have the four levels to give a basis for transcendental method, but we have all the possibilities of the differentiations of consciousness, of the realms and stages of meaning, of the brands of common sense, of the forms of conversion, to give the rich play of history.

LONERGAN'S CONTRIBUTION (3): THE GENERALIST PRINCIPLE

System and history deal respectively with the universal and the particular, but an integrating mind must deal with both; integration is a concept that transcends the universal/particular division. A useful term in which to speak of this, one that Lonergan himself favoured, is 'generalist'—it avoids the unwelcome connotation of mere logic that we might find in the kindred term 'universal'. Lonergan may sometimes use 'general' and 'universal' interchangeably, but the context will show that in that case 'universal' does not mean the concept cut off from its source in understanding—that would be the conceptualism he had so resolutely opposed early in life.

Lonergan remained strongly generalist all his life, even after he had worked out his categories for the scholarship which deals with the particular. In preparation for a congress of Jesuits teaching philosophy he had been sent a questionnaire that provided an outlet for his ideas on this topic: future professors of philosophy must 'come to understand how arduous is their task. They are to be generalists.'[1]

His own practice provides outstanding examples of his theory. 'The form of inference' (1943) proposes to find the 'general form of all inference'.[2] In *Insight* (1953) empirical method becomes a 'generalized' empirical method which includes the data of consciousness as well as the data of sense.[3] In fact, running through the book with this question in mind, we can gather a lot of data on Lonergan's passion for generalizing. 'Even more fundamental than scientific collaboration is scientific generalization';[4] Darwin's natural selection is a 'particular case of a more general formula';[5] common sense 'is common without being general';[6] it has its 'generalizations' but they are not like the generalizations proposed by science;[7] dialectic is 'a pure form with general implications . . . the general form of a critical attitude';[8] and so on.

What allows us to join knowledge of the particular case to knowledge of the systematic is the act of understanding—always we come back to that—which pivots between the concrete and the abstract, between the particular and the general. In the first instance this occurs in an upward movement from the particular, but thereafter it can occur in a downward movement from the formed concept to a particular application. That application is by no means a merely mechanical step. Its complexity appears in interdisciplinary procedures, where philosophers play the role of intermediary. But:

> it cannot be stressed too strongly that the mediation of the generalists is intelligent rather than logical: by logical mediation I understand the process from universal concepts to particular instances as just instances; by intelligent mediation I understand the process from understanding the universal to understanding the particular. The difference between the two is a difference in understanding: in logical mediation one understands no more in the instance than one did in the universal; in intelligent mediation one adds to the understanding of the universal a fuller and more determinate understanding of the particular case. The generalist that is just a logical mediator turns out to be an obtuse intruder; the generalist that is an intelligent mediator speaks not only his own mind but also the language of his interlocutor.[9]

LONERGAN AS PHILOSOPHER-THEOLOGIAN-METHODOLOGIST

Lonergan's integrating and generalist approach gives us a fair notion of what a philosophy worked out according to his ideas might look like. It also gives us a start on what a 'theology according to Lonergan' might look like, for theology uses general categories as well as those special to itself. Thirdly, the fourfold structure of human consciousness, with its two directions of development, gives us the structure of transcendental method in general and of theological method in particular with its eight functional specialties, each of which is illuminated by the general categories it employs. Thus, the preceding sections supplement what we have already said on the three intertwining areas of philosophy, theology, and methodology.

If, in this final chapter, we are to consider Lonergan's overall contribution under these headings, I suppose it is stating the obvious to say that his achievement on the level of the times lies primarily in the instrument he created for doing philosophy and theology, and only secondarily in the philosophy and theology that he himself produced.

This applies especially to his own specialization of theology. He was not a 'now' theologian, as so many of his justly honoured contemporaries were. He had a different and more austere vocation: deliberately to set aside the provision of immediate answers to present questions, to aim at a more distant target, to build for the future. Over and over there returns to me in this context what Karl Jaspers has said: 'For more than a hundred years it has been gradually realized that the history of scores of centuries is drawing to a close'.[10] The implications of such a view are staggering, but it is only by taking stock of them that we can make a true estimate of what Lonergan was about, for he worked all his life as if he were preparing for that new 'axial' period that—so Jaspers seems to suggest —we are now entering. We must therefore grant first place in his contribution, his *apport*, to the organon he constructed, and that has certainly been done in the present study. But it would be an egregious failure if I overlooked the profound rethinking he did on some of the most basic problems of theology, and of the way new ideas are grafted onto old branches in his courses and writings.

There is, in fact—I digress for a moment—the strangest mixture of old and new in the theological notes he produced through a quarter of a century in the classroom. In some degree this is to be expected; it could hardly have been otherwise. No one was more respectful of what his namesake, Bernard of Chartres, had said centuries before: we are pygmies standing on the shoulders of giants; no one was more keenly aware that standing there we can see farther than even the giants did, and must plot our course accordingly; with other progressive–conservative theologians, he struggled to bring out of his storehouse new things and old. But this combination has an especially incongruous character in Lonergan. One reason is clear enough: slower to change course than were most of his contemporaries, he kept to traditional paths in his teaching; possibly, there is a second reason in his farsighted vision of Church and world heading into a more distant future. The two may be paradoxically related: because his view of the coming revolution in theology was more radical, he needed more time to prepare for it, and meanwhile clung more cautiously to old forms.

In any case we have in his Latin theology that strange combination of outmoded elements—language, style of argument, seminary context—with the most profound rethinking on topics of engrossing contemporary interest: the law of the cross, the consciousness of Jesus, the three divine Subjects in their community, the social order of the people of God, and so on. It is a case again of new wine in old bottles, and the new wine, as happened in the Middle Ages, is a new conceptuality for which the old is an inadequate container.

An outstanding example is Lonergan's work in *De constitutione Christi ontologica et psychologica* on the consciousness of Christ. The data are the data of the old faith: that Jesus suffered, could say 'I thirst', and so on. But the thinking is the thinking of *Insight*, where experience, understanding, judgement, consciousness and knowledge, insight and introspection are worked out in a coherent pattern of relations. I know of no single work that is at once so topical, so penetrating, and so completely disregarded by established currents of thought as Lonergan's study of the consciousness of Christ.

Let me take another example where the pattern worked out in *Insight* has not yet been applied: the theology of the Holy Spirit present and active among us. This, in my view, is far and away the most monstrous omission of contemporary ecclesial life, doctrine, and practice. How account for the neglect? I suggest as a cause the lack of a conceptuality that can unite the outward, organizational, institutional with the inward, mystical, quickening element. This again could be provided by *Insight* with its generalized empirical method that unites the data of sense with the data of consciousness. That notion, abstract though it may appear, could be basic for relating the Johannine 'what our ears have heard, what our eyes have seen, what our hands have touched' with the Pauline 'harvest of the Spirit . . . love, joy, peace, patience . . .'. It would be only a beginning, a first step on the way to a Church in which discernment takes equal rank with power, but it remains unexploited while we drift in the current of an unacknowledged behaviourism.

I would adduce a third example of a great need in the Church that study of *Method* would go a long way to meet. A century ago we had a crisis of scholarship, in which we were trying vainly to teach that Moses wrote the Pentateuch, to take one of a hundred examples. Today we are going through a crisis of *aggiornamento*, in which we are trying, likewise vainly, to overcome the opposition to Pope

John's leap forward, *un balzo innanzi*. What *Method* could bring to both crises is a sense, through the pattern of eight functions set out in Chapter 5 above, of what is going on: of the role of research, interpretation and history in studying our past, of the role of dialectic and foundations in finding our own present, above all of the interlocking relations of function with function and mediating functions with mediated.

I mention these few sample headings from Lonergan's philosophy and theology, without being able to go into the content of either branch in any detail. It was important to do so, because it is important not to think of Lonergan merely as a methodologist in philosophy and theology, or as a philosopher–theologian working out a methodology for his field (for there is a hermeneutic circle and mutual mediation in this relationship). As a further preventative of this misconception I would notice some particular contributions in the field where Lonergan's work is least known, that of practice: for example, in moral thought, and very specifically in economics.

His views on moral theology are at the most fundamental level— of course; where else would we look? The foundation of moral precepts is discovered, not in some most general enunciated axiom, but in the very dynamism of intentional human consciousness; one moves from 'is' to 'ought', not in virtue of some logical implication but in virtue of a principle prior to principles, in the power of an intentionality that cannot rest with what is, but asks what is to be done. In consequence, Lonergan's moral theology is a theology primarily of responsibility, not primarily of rights; it is a theology that primarily seeks the good, not primarily one of negative precepts. Furthermore, because human consciousness is historical, ever learning from and correcting the past to determine a new future, therefore the hegemony of law would yield to the hegemony of a concrete apprehension of the human good effected through a theory of history:

If at one time law was in the forefront of human development . . . at the present time it would seem that the immediate carrier of human aspiration is the more concrete apprehension of the human good effected through such theories of history as the liberal doctrine of progress, the Marxist doctrine of dialectical materialism and, most recently, Teilhard de Chardin's identification of cosmogenesis, anthropogenesis, and christogenesis.[11]

131

A particular but still very broad question for this line of thought is the relation between theology and the human sciences; it will lead us to Lonergan's study of economics and explain why he thought that important for moral theology. A paper he wrote for the International Theological Commission is called 'Moral theology and the human sciences'. Here he proposed to speak first of

> human science as science, and so treat its empirical principle. Secondly . . . human science as human, and so there is considered its dialectical principle. Thirdly, there is the concrete realization of both the empirical and the dialectical principle in the ongoing scientific community. So it is only in the fourth place that we come to Catholic Action, or under favorable circumstances, Christian Action, which operates beneficently both on the human community to which human sciences are applied and on the scientific community that develops and revises the human sciences.[12]

There are three cases to consider. In one 'neither the science . . . nor its possible applications are in doubt'; in the second, the science 'is not sufficiently determinate to yield fully concrete applications'; but in the third the 'human science is itself open to suspicion. Its representatives are divided ideologically . . . The notorious instance at the present time is economics.'[13]

So we come to the economics that pre-empted his last years of life, as it had been a concern of his youth. I have mentioned the interest of the early Lonergan in current affairs: it shows up in his student writings during the 1930s, it reappears in the brief articles and reviews he did for the local press while teaching theology in Montreal in the 1940s. The particular interest in economics goes back at least to the early 1930s:

> When I came back to Canada in 1930, the rich were poor and the poor were out of work . . . Many theories were floating around. I was interested in Social Credit; I knew it would be inflationary if the banks dished out twenty-five dollars to everyone in the country every payday. Still, what was wrong with their argument? You had to understand the dynamic of events.[14]

Once more Lonergan refuses to stay in the ivory tower to which some of his critics would banish him: economics is part of his intellectual apostolate. People are suffering; there is a pastoral need to be met. Further, you don't meet the problem except by an adequate theory of economics: 'if you want to give moral advice to an economist, you have to know how the economy runs'.[15] There was a Catholic precept that employers must pay a family wage, but Lonergan's approach was through economic moral precepts that are based on the economy itself, not on the extrinsic base of family needs.[16] Implicit in these two points is the view that economic questions have theological implications; in fact, when Lonergan returned late in life to his early interest, he called his course 'Macroeconomics and the dialectic of history', and of course the dialectic of history is a theological question through and through.

Lonergan was still working on his economics at Boston College in March 1983 when his active career came to an end; he could no longer cope with the multiple troubles from which he would die in November 1984. Whether or not his work in economics will prove to be a significant contribution is a question I must leave to the experts. My concern has been to show how it fits in the pattern of his lifework. I think we can see that it is integral in a way the examples of mathematics and science in *Insight* were not: those were just instances of the way the human mind worked on the level of intelligence; in the economics he is far more deeply involved, it is a fourth-level responsibility.

THE LONERGAN MOVEMENT: ITS FUTURE, ITS PRESENT

What kind of future has the Lonergan movement, as it is beginning to be called?—A question provoked as much by the antics of his disciples as by the stonewall opposition of his critics. For me, however, the question has a more personal aspect: it is impossible to spend 44 years in intense study without speculating on the value of that study—which for me means forming a view on Lonergan's place in history.

My first remark is that on the spectrum of historical importance the future will assign Lonergan a place either toward one end or the other, but will not leave him in the middle. He will turn out to be either very much more than his critics now allow or very much less than his followers judge him to be. I do not see him taking a mediocre place in history. If he is less than we think him to be, he will be very much less, and will disappear from the headings of history to become only an obscure footnote. Similarly, if he turns out to be more than his critics allow, he will be very much more, giving a radical turn to theology, philosophy, the human sciences and human studies in general. I suppose it is obvious that my view is the latter, and I believe the evidence supports my view, though with Professor Fred Lawrence I will say that we do not really know how great Lonergan is.[17]

If we wish to be more 'objective' on this question we have first to ask on what basis one could evaluate such a thinker. One could, of course, collect the data on the reception he has received: strong advocacy on one side, strong opposition on the other. But the data have to be evaluated in their turn. What does the strong opposition mean? Resistance is to be expected if he is really a thinker of powerful originality; besides, though it is a mark against him in its content, it is a mark for him in its performance—it means that at least he is worth noticing. Oddly then, the more effective opposition comes from the silence of those who do not engage him but simply ignore him; circumstances, however, go a long way to account for this: an unknown from an unknown country teaching so long in an unknown tongue—the leaders in world-historical thinking would not expect to learn anything from that source. Neither, on the other side, should we assign his place in history on the basis of loyal discipleship in the Lonergan movement; as performance, it is ambivalent: naturally, a great thinker will have followers, but naturally too lesser minds will easily put their leader on too high a pedestal; as for content, that too has to be evaluated, and the wheat separated from the chaff. For the point applies to followers as well as to opponents, that, if Lonergan really is a giant, they too will be incapable of getting hold at once of his thought and locating him with accuracy in history.

So we await the verdict of time. Nor need we do more; it is only journalists who need instant evaluation, so that they can headline the greatest book of the decade, the greatest thinker of the century, and so on. In academe we must wait, and meanwhile we accept or reject Lonergan according to our own experience of thrilling to the power of his ideas, or failing to do so. My own task, so I have believed for some years, is not to argue with critics but to give myself as fully as possible to the study of his thought, primarily in research and interpretation, to a lesser extent in history, lesser still in dialectic. It happens that that is also my intellectual joy, so I live in peace with the opposition.

This now leads directly to a recurring charge: that we 'Lonerganians' do not talk to others, but form a clan of those who talk only to one another. There are data to support the charge: namely, that there is only sporadic discussion across the border with other schools or currents of thought. But it has to be said that the isolation is as much the creation of one side as the other: what possible conversation can a Lonergan student have with those who write work after work on understanding, and even hold congresses on the topic, but do not even list *Insight: A Study of Human Understanding* in the bibliography? Or with a theologian who dismisses Lonergan simply by saying he is a philosopher? With a philosopher who justifies setting Lonergan aside on the ground that he is a theologian? Or with the vanguard who think him hopelessly conservative? Or with the hopelessly conservative who label his work heretical? I think of the Protestant minister who told me in an ecumenical discussion: 'We didn't leave the Roman Catholic Church, we were pushed out' —one may respectfully suggest that at times followers of Lonergan feel pushed out too.

In my view, however, such charges and countercharges do not get to the nub of the question. I believe that, even if we talked across the boundaries to other 'schools', we would have little to say to one another: the Lonergan idea is too different, too revolutionary, too difficult, for easy conversation. There is a pertinent indication of that: the fact that the Lonerganians themselves do not really talk to one another! In view of all the Lonergan congresses that have been held in the last twenty years, this seems an outrageous statement, but it has a solid grain of truth and gives us a clue to the real situation: we are all of us 'reaching up to the mind' of Lonergan; each has reached a plateau but at different levels and on different sides of the mountain of his thought; we talk from our several plateaus and relate what we have discovered, but mostly we are too far apart for the talk to issue in conversation. That helps us understand also the reluctance of 'outsiders' to undertake the kind of study someone like myself has given Lonergan: who will start 44 years of study on one thinker without the inducement of a first encounter that captures their interest?

If I am right, then, we cannot hurry the process of the Lonergan movement; as I tell his impatient younger students, 'If you want instant results, get out of the Lonergan business'. Or, as I ask those seeking advice on how to study him: 'What kind of study have you in mind? If you merely want to recognize his name in a list with others, I can suggest an hour's reading; if you wish to say something intelligent when his name comes up at a cocktail party, you should spend a couple of days on him; if you would locate him in history with some real understanding, you must give him a semester; but if your aim is to be a Lonergan scholar, you must make a career of it.' He himself used to say that one should not expect the most fundamental ideas to take root, to find response, for another century. He speaks of weekend celebrities with something less than enthusiasm:

> To learn thoroughly is a vast undertaking that calls for relentless perseverance. To strike out on a new line and become more than a week-end celebrity calls for years in which one's living is more or less constantly absorbed in the effort to understand.[18]

So what can one suggest to those who are willing to make a start in the study of this difficult thinker? A great deal of patience, a modicum of humility, an ordinary dose of the charity that would rather save my neighbour's proposition than destroy it (Ignatius Loyola). A modicum of humility for openness to the idea that maybe there is something to learn from Lonergan; the ordinary minimal charity that checks my immediate dismissal of an author as uttering sheer nonsense—as can happen when 'the author [is] speaking of P and the reader [is] thinking of Q'. Then a useful distinction comes into play

> between the interpreter and the controversialist. On his mistaken assumption that the author is speaking of Q, the controversialist sets about his triumphant demonstration of the author's errors and absurdities. But the interpreter considers the possibility that he himself is at fault. He reads further. He rereads. Eventually he stumbles on the possibility that the author was thinking, not of Q, but of P, and with that correction the meaning of the text becomes plain.[19]

Patience is required, then, to persevere in a difficult task. There are introductions (like the one you are now reading) through which one may acquire in a day that acquaintance with current thought that cultured persons desire. But such books do not make a Lonergan scholar; better to turn to people who could design a guided reading course in Lonergan himself, one adapted to the place where the learners are and the distance they may wish to go. But beware: you might well find, when you have budgeted a semester of time to the project, that you are hooked for life!

CONCLUSION

I began this book with a remark on the need of a biography to provide a context for this and any other introduction to the work of Bernard Lonergan. I return in my conclusion to that need. For Lonergan was not a brain that issued thoughts; he was a person who was born, lived and died with the rest of us, and it is in the context of his life that we will best understand his work. While we await the biography (hopeful that it will not be long delayed) we may find profit in his notion of summation, and what the term means in the context of a human life.

There is, he says, a summation of intentional acts that is more familiar to us than the acts themselves: it is human living. Linked with it are, first, the summation of the objects of our acts into situations, into a world; and next, the summation of subjects into a 'we' who live together and perform the operations of life not singly, like so many isolated monads, but as a 'we'.[20] And later in the same lecture he returns to the topic to add: 'Destiny is perhaps the working out of individual autonomy within community, and so the summation of destinies in a community is the history of the community'.[21]

Here we have, ready-made, a scheme for a work on Bernard Lonergan: his life, as a summation of his activity through close to 80 years; his world, which is the world as he saw it, organized or chaotic, immediately of course a world of ideas, but of ideas intelligently grasped and reasonably affirmed to give it objectivity; and, finally, his community, the community into which he was born, in which he was nourished, which his lifework was meant to serve; and the subcommunity of the 'Lonergan movement' which has come into being as a result of that lifework.

The notion of summation was almost certainly taken from mathematics, in which Lonergan had so profound an interest; there it belongs to the integrating procedures of calculus, as contrasted with the procedures of differentiation. But there is a general sense of the term, which will be quite sufficient for our purpose, which is to point to the need we have for a study of the life and work and destiny within his community of Bernard Lonergan.

I do not think Lonergan 'planned' his life, though reference to an early interest in method might suggest that. He had an early dream of the *pantōn anakephalaiōsis*, and he pursued it for many years, but he allowed circumstances (and his superiors) to direct him: One step enough for me. There is evidence for this in the 'eleven years of

137

my life' in which he turned aside from direct pursuit of the dream, establishing a solid base in Thomas Aquinas, drawn perhaps by the delight in truth and love of it that he ascribes to Thomas,[22] 'admirabili delectatione et amore veritatis', but not foreseeing clearly where it was leading him. I suspect his analysis of the way Thomas worked became for him a model for his own procedure:

> There is a disinterestedness and an objectivity that comes only from aiming excessively high and far, that leaves one free to take each issue on its merits, to proceed by intrinsic analysis instead of piling up a debater's arguments, to seek no greater achievement than the inspiration of the moment warrants, to await with serenity for the coherence of truth itself to bring to light the underlying harmony of the manifold whose parts successively engage one's attention. Spontaneously such thought moves towards synthesis, not so much by any single master stroke as by an unnumbered succession of the adaptations that spring continuously from intellectual vitality. Inevitably such a thinker founds a school, for what he builds is built securely, and what the span of mortal life or the limitations of his era force him to leave undone, that none the less already stands potentially within the framework of his thinking and the suggestiveness of his approach. Finally, the greater such a genius is, perhaps the more varied will be the schools that appeal to him; for it is not to be taken for granted that the ever lesser followers of genius will be capable of ascending more than halfway up the mountain of his achievement or even, at times, of recognizing that one mountain has many sides.
>
> Such was the stamp of Aquinas . . .[23]

I know no better words in which to express my view on what Lonergan kept before him as his ideal and as a 'plan' for his lifework.

Very early in this study I spoke of the self-transcendence that is an integral element in his thought. I believe it is in place to draw attention in concluding to the degree of personal self-transcendence involved in responding to such a vocation as his was: to withdraw from the hunt when there is a quarry immediately before one, to give oneself to the forging of a new instrument, a *novum organum* for a new age, to be willing to spend one's entire life at the task with no certainty of success, with the single certainty that one's efforts will not, and in the nature of things cannot, be appreciated, this is no mean act of self-transcendence.[24]

Notes

1   B. Lonergan, 'Questionnaire on philosophy', *Method: Journal of Lonergan Studies* 2/2 (October 1984), p. 32.

2   B. Lonergan, in *Collection* ed. F.E. Crowe and R.M. Doran (2nd edn; *Collected Works of Bernard Lonergan* 4; Toronto, 1988), p. 4.

3   B. Lonergan, *Insight: A Study of Human Understanding* (2nd edn; London/New York, 1958), p. 243.

4   Ibid., p. 28.

5   Ibid., p. 132.

6   Ibid., p. 175.

7   Ibid., p. 176.

8   Ibid., p. 244.

9   B. Lonergan, 'Questionnaire', pp. 32–3.

10   K. Jaspers, 'The limits of educational planning' in *Philosophy and the World: Selected Essays* (Chicago, 1963), p. 22.

11   B. Lonergan, 'The transition from a classicist world-view to historical-mindedness' in *A Second Collection*, ed. W. Ryan and B. Tyrrell (London/Philadelphia, 1974/1975), pp. 6–7.

12   B. Lonergan, 'Moral theology and the human sciences', unpublished paper prepared for the International Theological Commission (the accompanying letter is dated 28 February 1974), p. 2.

13   Ibid., p. 1.

14   P. Lambert, C. Tansey and C. Going (eds), *Caring about Meaning: Patterns in the Life of Bernard Lonergan* (Montreal, 1982), p. 31.

15   Ibid., p. 225.

16   Ibid., p. 31.

17   F. Lawrence, ' "Cor ad cor loquitur": Bernard Lonergan, S.J.', *Compass: A Jesuit Journal* (*Special Issue Honouring Bernard Lonergan S.J. 1904–1984*; Spring 1985), p. 19.

18   B. Lonergan, *Insight*, p. 186.

19   B. Lonergan, *Method in Theology* (London/New York, 1972), p. 158.

20   B. Lonergan, 'The mediation of Christ in prayer', *Method: Journal of Lonergan Studies* 2/1 (March 1984), p. 9.

21   Ibid., p. 12.

22   B. Lonergan, *Grace and Freedom: Operative Grace in the Thought of St. Thomas Aquinas*, ed. J.P. Burns (London/New York, 1971), p. 145.

23   Ibid., p. 140.

24   I condense here what I said in the first chapter of *The Lonergan Enterprise* (Cambridge, MA, 1980).

Index

140